Call Back Yesterday

People of Lincolnshire remember the war

an anthology of personal memories
selected and edited by
Owen T Northwood

O, call back yesterday, bid time return,
And thou shalt have twelve thousand fighting men!
SHAKESPEARE *King Richard the Second*

Published by
Lincolnshire Books

Lincolnshire Books
1995
Official Publishers to

Lincolnshire County Council
Recreational Services
County Offices
Newland
Lincoln
LN1 1YL

Copyright © Owen T Northwood 1995

ISBN No. 1 872375 20 0

Printed by
Melton Printers of Lincoln
Industrial Unit No. 3, Sleaford Road
Bracebridge Heath, Lincoln LN4 2NA

Contents

Cover illustration.   Bomb damage to Stuart Street, Grantham, the morning after the air raid of 24 October 1942, from a pastel by Walter Lee. By permission of Grantham Museum.

Preface

Selecting and editing the material for this anthology of wartime memories has been no easy task. All of the events happened at least fifty years ago and during a time of danger and deprivation, yet the freshness and immediacy of recall does not generally indicate a wish to forget – indeed in some cases a particular sound such as thunder or breaking glass prompts the comment that it seems like only yesterday.

From the very large number of contributions received I have tried to choose excerpts which I think best portray what it was really like to live through a time of 'total war' and yet still try to live as normal a life as possible. The period covered starts in August 1939, just before war was officially declared and ends in August 1945. The selection is, inevitably, my own personal choice.

Acknowledgements

My thanks are due to everyone who helped with this book, and especially to all those 'People of Lincolnshire' who recalled their experiences so clearly; to Andrew Davies and staff at the Museum of Lincolnshire Life; to Terry Hancock, Julie Button and Faith Hopkins from Lincolnshire Library Service; to staff of Church Farm Museum Skegness, Kesteven Area Libraries and Grantham and Stamford Museums all of whom collected material for their own exhibitions and generously made it available to me, especially Pauline Walker at Stamford Library and Linda Carlisle at Grantham Museum who were my main points of contact and patiently answered my queries; to Neil French and Peter Waltham of Lincolnshire Archives for photographic expertise and excellence; to John Smith for suggesting the picture used on the cover and to Helen Ruthven for the cover design; to Mike Squire for help with layout and printing; to Sir Henry Nevile for his thoughtful introduction which also gave me the idea for one chapter heading; and to Tony Howlett for reading the text so critically and pointing out my typing errors!

Introduction ... *by Sir Henry Nevile* KCVO

Reading through some of the reminiscences in this collection – drawn mostly from Lincolnshire people – I am reminded of my own first connection with the War Effort.

In 1939 I enrolled briefly in the LDV (Local Defence Volunteers) and duly reported for duty at the top of Wellingore Mill armedwith my shotgun, where we waited to shoot the expected German parachutists as they floated down! Of course none came, but the memory stays with me as a reminder of our unpreparedness for war and of the amateurish way in which we set about defending our Country.

The stories in this book, in all their various ways, describe a time when we were younger – and perhaps more naïve – but when we all, whether in the Forces at home or overseas, or as civilians either in or out of uniform, had one aim in common, namely 'to get the war finished'.

I hope that this little book will remind my contemporaries of a time which, though often sad or frightening, was also full of fun and a time when lasting friendships were made.

I hope, too, that it will be of interest to the rising generation and help them to understand why we have felt it so important to celebrate VE and VJ days.

I wish the book every success.

Merchant Navy Larks...

"Coffee is served. Sir."

When we were young ...

The onset of war brought a new dimension to many young lives, often disrupting them severely and childhood, a time which should have been pleasant and carefree, became frighteningly dangerous for some children. The simple things of life were however still important and are recalled along with the serious and sad, which are an inevitable consequence of war.

*

September 3 was a beautiful sunny morning.   I stood in the back doorway with my Mam and Auntie Flo and heard Prime Minister Neville Chamberlain tell us that we were ' ... in a state of war with Germany'.   I was very frightened as I expected us to be overwhelmed by shooting, killing, enemy soldiers.   It wasn't a bit like that.   Life seemed to go on but with big changes.   We were issued with Ration Books and had to learn to manage on less.   Being a child at school, those worries were not mine!   So I tried my gas mask regularly (ugh! it was awful) and we had air-raid drill at school where the whole crowd of us squeezed under the concrete staircase as there were no shelters built yet.   I moved to a new school and during air raids our teachers kept us busy singing rounds.   Who remembers *My Dame hath a Lame Tame Crane*? On the lighter side, we had a line painted along the outside of our shelters and practised tennis shots.

We had a rabbit club, as 'Rabbit keeping in wartime is not a hobby, it is a **craft**' said Mr Meech, the Chairman.   We knitted socks, balaclava helmets, scarves and gloves for the troops and collected scrap metal and paper to make munitions.   So many bus tickets used for somewhere in a bullet, we were told!

1

My brother in law who was in the Coldstream Guard sent me a big box of dates from North Africa and we sent him the *Beano* and *Dandy* and searched Grimsby for a decent nail-file – 7s 6d each and worth every penny for him.

Letters to and from loved ones were censored – and signed with large capital letters across the back.

ITALY   (I trust and love you)

HOLLAND   (Hope our love lasts and never dies)

XXX – BOLTOP   (Better on lips than on paper!)

Peg Francis,   Grimsby

The first thing I can remember about the war is queuing up with my parents and brother for my gas mask.   We were told that we must carry them with us at all times.   At school we had gas mask drill, the teacher would blow a whistle three times without any warning and we had to stop whatever we were doing and put our gas masks on.   If you forgot your gas mask you got your knuckles rapped.

Renee Shaw,   Willingham

The mournful sound of sirens will always stick in my mind; of the actual air raids I remember very little.   Our house had a coal cellar and I have a picture in my mind of being dressed in a siren suit and being quite cosy down there with my family.   At school we were taken to see the air-raid shelter.   This too must have been in a cellar and it was a very exciting place.   I was always hopeful that one day we might go there again, but we never did.

When we moved house my sister and I stayed at the same school.   It was a two mile journey made partly by bus going, and walking all the way home alone.   This was fraught with dangers for a small girl, the worst was having to pass a row of cottages with front doors opening straight onto the pavement. There was a letter 'G' on a post outside these and I believed that the whole row housed Germans and gave them as wide a berth as possible, but the road was not very wide. My sister had instructed me to dive for the ditch if a German aircraft went over and the pilot used me for shooting practice. So a considerable amount of the journey was spent choosing a suitable ditch and practising this life saving feat.

Very often a column of soldiers would be marching down our hill. They were usually singing and whistling and even a little girl of my size did not escape their eyes. It was very embarrassing. However I carried on, swinging my gas mask, wishing my parents had got me a Mickey Mouse model!

We settled into our new house with large garden. 'Digging for Victory' began in earnest and with the help of a great deal of fertiliser to break up the clay soil we began to produce potatoes, sprouts, beans *etc*. We started to keep hens, of whom I became very fond.

'We started to keep hens, of whom I became very fond.' Kath Marshall with Cheeky and Perky, 1945.

We were never short of eggs and my mother preserved, for winter, any excess eggs in a large earthenware bowl containing some white liquid. Christmas usually saw one of the beloved hens on the table, unrecognisable after the dressing and cooking.

Kath Marshall, Nettleham

Farmers were advised to make an air-raid shelter when possible in a strawstack or haystack that was not far from the house. Dad decided to do just that. A large square was cut out of the side of a haystack and over the entrance a very large old barn door was leaned against the hole, leaving two exits from the shelter. I can only remember actually going in this once or twice during air raids and us boys would play in it during the day. During one of these raids when we all got into the shelter with some of the farm workers and families one of the women said 'I shall have to go back to my house, I have forgotten to put my false teeth in'. Her husband shouted, 'Sit down you daft woman, it's bombs that they are dropping out there, not pork pies'.

We were later advised that this was not the safest of places to be at all. If the farmyard did get on fire and the haystack started to burn, we could all be asleep.

Dad was made the village air-raid warden and someone brought him his equipment. This consisted of a red tin lid with a hole in the centre and a four inch nail. When an air raid was announced he would get a telephone call and would be told one word only, 'Action'. He would then go and nail the red disc onto the village notice board which was on the farm building wall. On the all-clear he would go and take this warning down. After one trial run and one air raid this system seemed to become too lax and Dad would say, 'One of these days remind me to take that jolly lid down lads'.

One morning we woke up to find our fields covered with small yellow leaflets dropped by a German plane during the night. They contained many reasons why England should now surrender to the mighty Germans. We were not allowed to keep any and had to hand them in to the police. If only we had the time. Eventually the weather took care of them.

Dennis Fenwick, Beelsby

4

I was nine years old and my home was Poplar Farm, Croft where my father and brother, with help, farmed the 120 or so acres of mixed arable and dairying. Having been informed by the MOD or some such organisation that we were to be hosts to the army, it was no surprise to them when one breakfast time up rolled an army lorry with ten soldiers and an officer. Not having been discussed in my hearing the 'invasion' was a total surprise. On arrival the soldiers, who were all very young and newly recruited to the Leicestershire Regiment, quickly had to erect tents to sleep in and various holes soon appeared for gun emplacements, sewage, rubbish *etc.* Quite soon a searchlight appeared and they were in business. We were always awakened by the activity on the site as the generator was so close to the house and I remember my sister

'The soldiers were given permission to help.' (from right) Enid Kisby's father Fred Frith (3rd), sister Mavis (2nd) and brother Martin (7th).

and I peeping between the blackout curtains and seeing the searchlight beams lighting up the sky – and also our house.

Later in the war, when there was a quiet spell, the soldiers were given permission to help lead in the harvest with the army lorry and with other farm work. This was a novelty for both them and us.

Enid Kisby,   Wainfleet St Mary

During the war, as a child, I used to have little jumble sales for the 'Telegraph Tobacco Fund'. They used to send cigarettes to the Forces.

My father, although not fit enough to join the Forces, spent much of the war working on damaged aircraft for De Havilland and A V Roe. He was home for Christmas 1944, mainly for a rest as he was not too well. He enjoyed being with the family. My 13th birthday was on 1 January and we had a party on 6 January which the grown-ups enjoyed as much as the children. After it was over my dad said he could just eat some fish that his pal had brought him. I remember that mother bewailed the fact that it was late but nevertheless cooked it for him. It was to be the last meal she cooked for him. The next day he had a massive haemorrhage and died. I do remember.

Thelma Sadler,   Grimsby

At Westgate school, when the first air-raid shelter was built all of us had to run home and back to see who lived nearest, as there was only limited accommodation in it and it was to be used for those who lived furthest away. We seemed to spend many hours in the school shelter while the teacher read to us from *The Wind in the Willows*. For some unknown reason we never got past the first half, probably because the raids eased off.

Gordon Wing,   Lincoln

There were so many memories:

- The walk to school along Nettleham Road, picking pieces of bark off the old trees, ready to whittle into boats with my new penknife,

- the weekly pocket money spent by two ten year old adults in short trousers on a few chocolate liqueurs,

- sailing on a boat up the river from Brayford Pool, only a small boat but with so few in those days we really felt 'someone',

- punishment for our misdemeanours from our foster father's scratchy beard rasping our soft cheek but, as compensation, the

6

weekly pile of out-of-date comics brought by him from his newspaper workplace and for which we paid a nominal one penny,

• and the highlight of the week, Saturday afternoon. My parents had also been evacuated to Lincolnshire and we met up in Lincoln for a couple of hours a week to buy clothes, to talk and to have tea, always in the Bridge Café and always egg and chips.

Alan Hunter, Grimsby

My father and my Aunt Violet worked long shifts in the nearby steelworks. As the war years lengthened the steelworkers put on Christmas parties to keep up morale among the workers' children. We were taken right into the heart of the steelworks, past the huge furnaces and rollers, onto the metal plate area for our entertainment. One Christmas present I received from my aunt was a doll's cradle, made Meccano fashion, from strips of steel and decorated with some flimsy material, probably parachute leftovers. It brought great joy in those austere days of rationing.

Thelma Robinson, Gainsborough

We had to get used to fitting the blackout at home and walking in the winter evenings without any street lights, and only a torch to help. When air-raid warnings came at night we retreated to the pantry which was deemed the safest spot and outside of which a blast wall had been built. We sat on two flour tins and the bread tin. Sticky tape had been stuck over the French windows at the back and above, in the bedrooms, the net curtains had been stuck to the glass.

One night a German bomber returning home dropped three bombs near us. The crash woke us up and we went downstairs, my mother thinking that the light coming through the blackout card over the glass in the front door was fire. The two semi-detached houses at the bottom of our garden had been hit, the nearest being almost completely demolished. Our bedroom window had been

'Perhaps the net curtains saved my brother's life.' Douglas Boyce, with brother Allan in the wheelbarrow, October 1940.

smashed and perhaps the net curtains had saved my brother's life, sleeping in the cot below the window. Looking out of the window I asked about the house at the end of the road which had wallpaper on the outside. We then realised that another three houses had been demolished.

Sometimes my grandfather would take me out for a walk. We always went down Sandy Lane where I was invited to put my hand inside a hollow tree. I was always too scared to put it in far so my grandad had to reach in and bring out the peppermints which were always there.

Douglas Boyce, Market Rasen

Grimsby became full of servicemen in all kinds of uniform. Bell bottoms of the RN, khaki battledress of the army and lots of airforce blue. Later on the Yanks arrived. Their privates' uniforms were as well tailored as our officers' and their officers were lavishly outfitted. Many English and American personnel were billeted in empty houses in the town. Black Americans were billeted in the People's Park and some of them were extremely handsome. In the evenings the park was full of them and local girls. They were an exotic addition to restricted wartime life.

The American Red Cross took over a building in Old Market Place and some houses nearby. We heard stories of how the sheets were changed every day. Food and comfort unlimited; lots of money for taxis and spending on girls. Their MPs with their white 'snowdrop' helmets patrolled the night-time streets in high profile. If there was any trouble it was not heard about.

A few months after my brother was killed in the RAF we had a heavy air raid and emerged from the air-raid shelter to find our house uninhabitable. All ceilings were down, all windows blown out, absolute chaos in every room. Our cat 'Geronimo' was safe but terrified in his basket in the outside wash house. Next morning, a sunny June day, my father had to go to the docks but I stayed off school, found some wood and nailed the front bay window up. One of my school friends came round at midday to find out how we were. It all seemed a great adventure to be standing there in the sunshine after our own 'little blitz' and carrying on as usual – just like in the newsreels.

Dorothy Johnson, Skegness

As children at the village school at Ulceby we learned the usual popular songs and also sang many others which magically just came from somewhere. The first song I can recall as a prelude to the war was:

> *Will you come to Abyssinia will you come?*
> *Bring your own ammunition and your gun.*
> *Mussolini will be there, shooting peanuts in the air,*
> *Will you come to Abyssinia will you come?*

– all quite meaningless to small Lincolnshire school children. Where was Abyssinia? – and who was Mussolini? Another song somewhat later was connected with the release of Walt Disney's Snow White, and went:

> *Whistle while you work,*
> *Snow White made a shirt.*
> *Hitler wore it, Goering tore it,*
> *Whistle while you work.*

– another verse included:

Goering's barmy, so's his army
Whistle while you work.

– it mattered little that Goering was in fact in command of the German airforce.

Tony Cawthorpe,   Skegness

As a boy of eleven I remember being quite excited when the Anderson shelter we had requested was finally delivered.   We lived very close to the sea in Cleethorpes and consequently the soil in our garden was light and sandy.   I helped my father dig a hole about three feet deep into which we erected the shelter, the spoil from the hole being used to cover the top of the shelter.   The tall dock tower at Grimsby was a good navigational aid to the German airmen and they frequently flew in over our town.   The very same night we finished the shelter the sirens sounded, searchlights stabbed the sky and a light ack-ack battery sited on the beach at the end of our street commenced firing.   I remember vividly being rudely awakened, rushing down the stairs, grabbing a coat off the hall stand and pulling it on over my pyjamas.   Mother was the first into the shelter and suddenly from within came a scream. Although my father had put a wooden floor into the shelter it was floating in about eighteen inches of water.   My father and I ran to the garden shed and fetched a pair of steps, empty boxes and anything else we could find so that we could stand clear of the water.

By now mother had lit a candle and as I was climbing into the shelter she was horrified to see that I was wearing her best coat over my pyjamas.   With a cry of anguish she said, 'Germans or no Germans, you can take my coat off and get your own!'.   So started the first of many nights spent in our shelter.   As for the water, what had happened of course was that the tide had come in and that had altered the water table, hence the flooded shelter.   We could only hope that Jerry would come over when the tide was out and the shelter dry!

Colin Mackenzie,   Cleethorpes

Leaving home ...

The government believed that cities would come under immediate attack from the air and made arrangements to evacuate children and some adults to less vulnerable parts of the country. They travelled to unknown destinations, and were not always welcome, yet many found it an exciting and interesting experience and some, even though sometimes they stayed for only a fairly short time, eventually formed lifelong friendships with their hosts.

*

Tuesday 29 August 1939.   A day by the sea, a day as any other, all the beach for a 10 year old boy to dig, with not a cloud in the sky.   But the next day the holiday had to be cut short to return to Leeds to prepare for evacuation.   Two days of washing, ironing, packing for Mum while I played, partly awaiting the adventure to come, partly apprehensive of the unknown.   Then reporting to Roundhay School on the Friday morning with suitcase in hand, gas mask in cardboard box over one shoulder, sandwiches in pocket, label round neck, ready for the long train journey to Lincoln.

On arrival we were taken by bus to a little school in St Giles' where we were issued with two days' emergency rations, and then on to the northern parts of the city, to be hawked around the houses in the Ruskin Avenue area at street-end mini slave markets.   It went on late, very late, into the summer's evening. Finally Vernon and I were taken in by a Mr and Mrs Wilden who reluctantly agreed to be my foster parents for a short while.

Sunday morning, 3 September, saw us exploring our new territory, being near the Cathedral when the bells struck eleven o'clock. I remember a hollow feeling in my stomach, wondering if this was a striking of doom. Back home we heard the worst. There had been no message from Germany so Britain was at war. That night was our first and only brush with the war in Lincoln. All safely in bed, at 2am the warbling sirens went and we were roused, made to dress and marched off up Nettleham Road to open fields where we were told to stand near the ditch. It didn't help being told by Mr Wilden that in the Great War only one Zeppelin dropped bombs on Lincoln and they fell quite near this field! Whether it was true or not we didn't know but it did nothing for our confidence! So we just stood and shivered until an hour later the all-clear came from the distance and we all trailed back, tired, cold, sleepy to our beds.

As Christmas approached there was increasing talk of where to spend the festive season. Would we risk going to Leeds, and if we did go home would we ever return to Lincoln? In the end our school had shelters built; no bombs had fallen on Leeds but were feared for Lincolnshire with its airfields. So Christmas stockings were hung up in Yorkshire and we all stayed for the remainder of, for us, a peaceful war.

Alan Hunter,   Grimsby

During the war we had to take evacuees from Leeds. I remember an elderly lady and her grandson came to us one day. She asked my mother if she could buy a chicken from her to boil to make soup. Mother caught a chicken for her but she would not let mother kill it. She went with it under her arm to Lincoln.

When she came back dad asked where she had been. She told dad she had been to the priest for him to kill the fowl for her, for which she was charged 6d. Dad said he would have done it for nothing; but the priest had to bleed it – dad said he could have done that; but the priest said a prayer over it and blessed it – dad said he could have done all that for nothing!

Florence Pearson,   Nettleham

One evening a train load of evacuees arrived at the station just below our house.   At the pre-arranged time my mother collected Peter from the Church Hall.   He was about ten years old and came from Plaistow, London.   He stayed with us for the duration of the war.

Peter soon integrated into village life and got into all sort of scrapes.   One afternoon he was making his way up the hill to our house when he was seen to stop, take out his clean hankie, and polish his boots before coming in.   *Just William* had nothing on Peter.

One Christmas his mother brought a present each for my brother and me.   My present was a special pencil which, as you turned the top, would allow you to use different colours.   It was a marvellous gift and I proudly took it on my Sunday afternoon walk.   Of course I lost it and was heartbroken for days.

Another walk Peter and I went on one day was along the mountainside to collect blueberries.   Unfortunately we had a summer shower and arrived home as blue as the berries from the cheap dye in our wartime clothes.   We were in trouble!!

Thelma Robinson,   Gainsborough

Our two evacuees were company although I admit to being quite frightened of the elder of the two, who arrived with filthy feet and the only clothes she had were the ones she stood up in. Mum soon remedied this but I still remember my heartbreak when she was given a cream and brown check coat with a brown velvet collar which was to have passed on to me from my sister.   They were treated just like us and sometimes better, I thought.   When

I asked God to bless them in my prayers each night I often felt hypocritical, especially of one. I found myself giving up my much treasured books which she would deliberately tear or drop on the floor, and I had to keep quiet because she was a long way from home!

Betty Cowley, Sturton by Stow

One morning we went to school with a suitcase containing clothes which we had been given, carried our gas masks, had a label pinned to our coats with our name and address on it and also had a stamped postcard, addressed to our parents, to fill in and send off when we got to where we were going. I was eight and my brother 10½ and we had never been away from our parents or out of London before. From school we marched to the railway station which was full of children waiting to be evacuated.

It was a very emotional time, the parents did not know where their children were going and just hoped they would be properly looked after by a kind hearted stranger. I was frightened and crying. My mother told me to cheer up as it would be like going on holiday, but I'd never been on holiday and if this was holiday I didn't want to know. I got onto the train with everyone else and off we went. By the time the train left it was dark and we could not see where we were going. It seemed a very long journey before we finally arrived in Bath. About 20 of us were put on a bus and taken to the village of Bathford. We were met at the village school by the billeting officers whose task it was to get us to our foster homes.

Each officer took about five children and walked down the dark lanes knocking on doors and handing children over. When he knocked on Mrs Yeates' door he was told 'Take the children somewhere else, I'm not having evacuees'. The billeting officer got very cross, told her there was a war on, there was plenty of room in her house and she was having two children. My brother and I were pushed into the house and we both felt scared. We were given something to eat and put to bed in separate rooms; that was quite a shock, it was a big bedroom and I had never slept on my own before, I'd always shared a room with my brother. I was so homesick I cried myself to sleep.

Renee Shaw, Willingham

I was six when the war started. My mother told me a little girl would be evacuated with us and that she would be a playmate for me. Being an only child I could hardly wait for her to arrive at our house in Browning Drive.

One morning when I came downstairs I found a young man, 15

years old, sitting at our breakfast table and my mother told me he was Paul Fitton, our new evacuee from Roundhay School in Leeds. I was so disappointed that he wasn't a girl I almost cried and I immediately made up my mind to have nothing to do with him and that I wouldn't speak to him, and I didn't for about a week. Eventually I realised he was a good playmate after all and we were to become the best of friends.

'I found a young man sitting at our breakfast table.' Paul Fitton, billeted with Arthur, Margaret and Pat Scoffins, 1939.

My mother told me some years later why

Paul had come to stay instead of the girl she had promised me. Apparently at about 11 o'clock one night a man had knocked on the door asking if we would take a boy from Leeds. My mother immediately said no and explained that she had requested a girl. However the man persuaded my parents to step outside to see how many boys they still had to find places for. They were never to forget the sight which met their eyes. About 30 boys sitting or lying on the pavement, some were even asleep – they had been trailing the streets of Lincoln all day looking for someone to take them in and they were all exhausted.

Paul stayed with us for about three months and then returned to Leeds.

He wrote to us that Christmas ...

> *Leeds 8,*
> *Tuesday, 17 December 1940*
>
> *Dear Mr and Mrs Scoffins,*
>
> *I have not heard from you for some time now but I presume no news is good news and hope that you have not been bombed and that Pat is no worse for her accident. I am sending Pat a book that Rosemary and I used to like very much, I hope it will please Pat as much as it pleased us ....*
>
> *Merry Christmas! Have you got your puddings and cakes made yet. Mother has made some cakes. She saved our butter rations for several weeks to put in them so we ought to have something to look forward to.*
>
> *Wishing you all the best for Christmas and the New Year.*
>
> *Love from,*
> *Paul*

... and continued to keep in touch afterwards.

Pat Sharp, Lincoln

The threat from above ...

For the first time ever the whole population suffered the dangers of war and even the most remote places were not beyond the range of enemy attack. The larger cities and towns with factories were prime targets and air-raid shelters provided reasonable protection from all but a direct hit. In smaller villages it was largely a matter of luck as to whether a stray bomb would hit houses or fields and casualties were few.

*

I can see it now. War was declared – I am 14 years of age. Dad started to dig a hole for our Anderson shelter. Excitement – we had a trial run – the sirens sounded and dad took the family, mum and dad and six children to sit in the hole in the garden. We went with the handbag with the insurance policies and a bag of biscuits which we ate until the all clear sounded and then we all went back to bed.

Norah Gough, Holbeach St John

On the afternoon of 31 October 1940 I was in class at St Martin's school, Stamford when suddenly the sound of machine-gun fire was heard above the voice of Mr Richmond, our Headmaster. The class must have looked startled because he calmed us down by saying, 'It's alright boys, it's one of ours', but when we went home we found out differently. It was in fact a German bomber, flying low down the Welland valley on its way to the coast, that was machine gunning the town. Several people had lucky escapes and it dropped a bomb which landed in a house in St Leonard's St. My father was

17

going up St Mary's Hill in a lorry at the time this was going on and actually saw the bomb leave the plane over the top of St Mary's Church. When this happened the plane shot up in the air, as father said, 'as if it was on a bit of elastic'.

I remember seeing a row of bullet holes in the plaster work of the two shops opposite the Town Hall and of going down St Leonard's St to see if we could see where the bomb had dropped, but as it had not gone off the area was evacuated and sealed off until it had been made safe.

One night after we had gone to bed the sirens sounded. We didn't bother too much; most nights nothing happened but this night was going to be different. Soon the sound of engines could be heard in the distance and they were coming nearer all the time. As they got closer you could tell they were German planes because the engine sound was different to ours. My parents said, 'come on, it's time to get up'. They had arranged shelter in our neighbour's house at times like this as they had concrete bedroom floors. We dressed quickly by torch light because with the blackout curtains up you couldn't see a thing.

As we went out of the house it was as light as day. Not only was it moonlight but the German planes were dropping flares on the way up the valley towards Leicester. We could see the planes clearly, row after row in vee formation, even the crosses on their wings. We just had to stand and watch for a few minutes. We spent the rest of the night in our neighbour's front room. I don't think anyone got much sleep that night wondering where so many planes were going. The next morning, before going half-asleep to school, we heard on the wireless that the target was Coventry and of the terrible damage and deaths its people had suffered.

Kenneth Plant,   Stamford

It was 4 May 1944, 11.45pm and we had just gone to bed when we heard cannon fire. I recognised it because I worked at MAP,

Grantham, making the 20mm Hispano cannon. I jumped out of bed, opened the window and peeped out just in time to see a terrific ball of flame and hear the noise of engines in full acceleration. I turned to my wife telling her it was a plane going to crash near to us, but by the time I had spoken it was down, no more than 60 yards across the street from where we lived at 43 Eastgate, Bourne. It crashed on the Butcher's Arms public house and killed all the occupants and some soldiers billeted opposite. One German airman was taken prisoner, two parachutes failed to open and the pilot was buried under the engine.

Roland Bristow, Bourne

'I actually saw a bomb bounce.'
Colin Mackenzie, 1937.

At the age of fifteen I became an apprentice joiner at Doigs shipyard in Grimsby, working on fast motor launches and wooden minesweepers. My home was about two miles from the dock and it was easy for me to get home for dinner on my bicycle. Returning to work one day I heard the unmistakable drone of an aircraft flying very low just behind me and then machine-gun fire. I fell off my bike and scrambled into a shop doorway thinking I would be late for work.

A lone Dornier aircraft was flying above the main Cleethorpes to Grimsby road. I actually saw a bomb, which the aircraft dropped, hit the road and bounce into the air again. It went straight through the first-floor window of a clock and watch repairer by the name of Bell close to the corner of Humber Street, which is one of the roads leading to the docks. Because the aircraft was so low the bomb had no time to attain a vertical position as it fell, hence the bounce off the road. Bell's frontage was blown out and I was lucky the bomb hadn't exploded on impact.

Colin Mackenzie,   Cleethorpes

My worst memory is of walking over broken glass after one of the worst nights of air raids in 1940/41. I still cannot stand the sound of breaking glass. Living in Hampstead, I did not experience the heavy blitzing of the east end. Our biggest danger was shrapnel falling after a burst of anti-aircraft fire from the battery on the Heath.

Grace Dawson,   Boston

I remember Mr Longbottom of Holland Fen, who was driving his tractor down the field when a bomb fell on him and killed him. I think it was a British bomb.

Nora Shaw,   Boston

We had a lucky night and escaped injury from German bombers. There was an unexploded bomb in the Glory Hole at the bottom of Water Lane [now Littlewoods store], then a tailor's business in the name of Curtis, my father-in-law. Incendiaries had also been dropped in the Cornhill area. My home was 38 Dixon Street. Bombs were dropped in the street and our house was the last one to be damaged. Hard core from the road came in through the roof onto my son's pillow. It was lucky we were not at home. We were told of the happenings in Dixon Street area so I borrowed my brother-in-law's bike and went to find out what had happened. When I got there two mates who lived in the street and played in the Salvation Army Band with me were boarding up my front bay window and door. I went back to Water Lane to find that they were all being evacuated from the area and we all went to 15 Newland Street West to my other brother-in-law's house, fifteen of us all told, we slept on sofas and chairs and the floor.

On another occasion I was working in daylight on a low roof at Syston near Grantham. A German bomber came peppering military vehicles down the park drive. I rolled down the roof into a heap of sand without mishap.

I was on duty with the Police Specials on Cross O'Cliff Hill when a land mine was dropped at the top. My partner pushed me in the back and we both fell flat on the ground on our front. We just had to brush ourselves down.

Harold Watts, Lincoln

I lived at Beeston near Nottingham, on a farm and on one occasion incendiaries fell all down our field setting the pigsty on fire. Whenever there was an air raid we went into the shelter and called our neighbours in, taking a bottle of elderberry wine with us.

Alice Gibson, Grantham

On Sunday 29 December 1940 I was home from school for the Christmas holiday. We had not celebrated Christmas Day as the whole family had not got together by then so we were all at home on that evening. The air-raid siren sounded the warning shortly after 6pm. The night was to develop into the second Great Fire of London.

Not having an air-raid shelter to retire to we continued with our meal. The first bomber droned over with the very characteristic fluctuating engine beat. Suddenly a thin whistling developed. It was my first bomb, whereas all the others had heard them before. We sat transfixed for what seemed like a minute then the bomb went off. It was about 150 yards away on the corner of the British Museum. The windows remained intact. Then we heard other smaller noises, more like thuds. My father sprang up and shouted 'incendiaries' and we all grabbed our hats and coats and filed out of the flat and downstairs to the basement where we awaited developments. Bombs could be heard and the drone of German aircraft. A lot of anti-aircraft fire was going up and fragments of the four-inch shells then rained down into the streets. After half an hour or so we went upstairs and out into the night.

In the street we stood looking up into the sky. It was almost as light as day; a reddish cast covered the sky; there was a smell of burning wood and large flakes of burnt paper slowly rained down. It became obvious to us that we were not the main target that night. The City and East End were receiving many tons of high explosive and incendiary bombs.

I walked down High Holborn in the morning to see the damage and watch the office workers and shop assistants arriving for 'business as usual'. Where buildings remained standing, as around Gamages and the Old Bailey, there was no glass in place. Shop windows were open to the elements. Hundreds of firemen stood around smoke blackened and exhausted and hoses snaked across the roads and ruins spraying everything in sight. People were clambering over mounds of rubble and using St Paul's churchyard as a route to their jobs. Opposite Gamages there was extra interest for the crowds as a bomb from the First World War was revealed jammed in a chimney and presumably dropped in a Zeppelin raid a quarter of a century earlier. It had remained undetected while years of coal fires had kept it warm!

Deryk Wakem, Deeping St James

We dug deep into our garden and put in an Anderson shelter, securing it with cement – where my father obtained this I don't know, such things were hard to come by – but as it turned out we had cause to be very thankful for this extra security. I was off duty that particular night in September when the Blitz was at its height. There were two neighbours plus their two young children, my mother and myself sharing the shelter when the land mine hit our home. That Anderson shelter rocked about as if it was a ship

22

being tossed about in a very stormy sea. What with that, three screaming women and two crying children I had my hands full. When things settled down we had to find the matches, candles and drinking flask, fortunately undamaged, and wait for rescuers to dig us out. Dirt and dust was everywhere – and our home was gone.

Margy Aitken, Skegness

On hearing the siren we had a routine. Mother collected the documents, I carried my sister's eldest, who was a toddler and the heaviest, and we made straight to sit either under the big table or under the stairs until the all clear went. Of course, once we had the Anderson shelter installed in the back garden we went there where we had bunk beds. I remember all of us being there all night once and coming out to see an incredible red glow in the sky from the direction of Hull where they had had an incendiary raid. We were lucky but our sirens still went. My father was an ARP Warden.

Joan Highfield

I worked at Aveling Barford munitions factory in Grantham.

'They bombed us quite a lot'
Ruby Clark, early 1945.

Even in 1945 we never thought the war would be over that year. So many men getting killed. The men and women came from all over the world to help us out. I had some good lodgings at Grantham. We were a friendly crowd who worked together.

They bombed us quite a lot. We always got under the stair-case. The bombs seemed to bounce. No wonder I am scared of thunder. There were several

23

people killed at Grantham. They were after the railway line. I often wonder who the cruel people were to show them a light. One thing, we never let them get us down. When the war ended there was dancing in the streets and parks and everyone was so excited. The wives were looking for their husbands coming home. People have no idea what a relief it was. We could get a good night's sleep without the bombing and sirens going. We are going to miss the cheerful voice of the ARP Warden calling 'All Clear' through the letter box.

Ruby Clark, Manby

The worst night was when our house was bombed. We were all in the shelter, except for dad who was on fire watching duties and we could tell by the noise that the raid was right overhead. Suddenly there was a terrific crump and the shelter moved sideways. A voice called out 'Are you alright?'. Mother replied 'Yes' and we were told to get out as it wasn't safe. We got out and found the house had received a direct hit and collapsed over the shelter. No time to stand and look as the raid was still going on. We were told to run 150 yards down the street where there was a shelter with room for us.

It was terrifying. High-explosive bombs were coming down with an ear-splitting whistle, houses were collapsing, fires burning fiercely, shrapnel flying about and people yelling. The noise was tremendous and breathing was difficult because of the smoke. We made it to the shelter and mother left us because she was a Red Cross nurse and was needed. We were glad to see her when the raid was over.

Renee Shaw, Willingham

In 1944 I was a Leading Wren on the permanent staff of the WRNS Training HQ where hundreds of recruits received their uniforms, endured basic training and were then posted to HM ships and shore depots at home and abroad. The conventional air raids heralded by a siren were now very infrequent. On a foggy late autumn Sunday I, with a small group of Leading Wrens, was eating lunch when the windows shattered and our eardrums burst with the pressure of an almighty blast! Instinctively we were on our feet, only to be thrown to the floor by the terrible and unseen force. A V2 rocket had exploded in the grounds of the REME barracks next door. Casualties were fewer than they might have been as it was the weekend, Thank God! Several ATS girls and soldiers were killed but our injuries seemed superficial. Within a few minutes we had dusted ourselves down, picked ourselves up and carried on with our duties.

"We dusted ourselves down, picked ourselves up, amd carried on.' Leading Wren Joan Brown, *HMS Pembroke*, February 1944.

What we hated most about this devilish weapon was the total lack of warning.

Joan Brown,   Skegness

Cliff came home on leave during the summer of 1941 and promptly got a caution from the MPs for wearing shoes with his uniform. It was a lovely day so we took a walk towards Winthorpe, Cliff proudly pushing the pram, when we heard gunfire above us and saw two German bombers being chased by two of our fighters. We hurried home and in the passageway to mother's garage we watched the dog fight. Our neighbours joined us and one said 'Look at those birds flying underneath that plane'. Of course they were the bombs which they scattered along the foreshore, as I remember, doing very little damage.

Lumley Road was bombed and the Tower Cinema was hit during a matinée. The bombs were not the weight of those in later years but Mr Morgan the accountant was killed.

One Sunday the church bells rang. This was prohibited except as a signal for invasion. The guns – which we presumed to be out at Candlesby – began to fire, rumour was rife. My brother who was working in Lincoln arrived on the doorstep. He had had a job to get to Skegness; on hearing the bells he had dashed to the bus station for a bus home. Three times during the journey from Lincoln the bus was stopped by the police who demanded that any passengers from Skegness had to get off. He sat still and made it home. All sorts of rumours abounded, ... there were barges at Gibraltar Point ..., but we never knew the truth.

Ena Taylor,   Skegness

I was walking along Windsor Bank, Boston when a plane dropped an oil bomb which blew me into Bargate Drain bank, just short of the water. I had difficulty clambering up the bank and found Windsor Bank a mass of flames. I could not walk with the damage to my hand and leg. A soldier, who had just returned from the Dunkirk beaches, insisted I should be sent to a First Aid post, so he started to look for one.

Arthur Acott,   Boston

I remember the sirens going off and having to take shelter in the outside toilet – and hoping I wouldn't die there!

Margaret Smith,   Lincoln

To war and arms we went ...

The armed forces built up rapidly, firstly through volunteers and later by conscription. Some people remained in the UK for the whole of their wartime service and were able to return home on leave at fairly regular intervals. Those posted abroad could be away for over four years with their family not knowing where they were, and whether they were safe, for a considerable period of time.

*

As the first rays of the sun fell, *HMS Reaper* raised anchor and moved slowly under the Forth Bridge and out into the North Sea. The *Reaper* had been for some little time loading captured foreign aeroplanes to take them over the sea to America. As the ship moved on down the east coast we met and turned into the English Channel. Our path took us along and across the Channel to the 'Pipe Line Under The Ocean'. This was code named 'Pluto' and brought fuel under the Channel to France, coming ashore at Cherbourg. Our exercise took advantage of 'Pluto'. As this came ashore with a surface pipe line well down the shore, our ship was able to pull in alongside the pipeline. We had here to load more planes to make the journey to America.

We set off across the Atlantic Ocean with a full load on the hangar deck and the flight deck. Each day we had an inspection of the planes under our command, to ensure that all was in order. We carried on to New York and tied up beyond the Statue of Liberty and work began unloading the planes right away. A floating crane of good size lifted the plane from the flight deck, over the dock and lowered it to the quay. A tractor then took over and towed the plane off the quay and away to safe storage. Each plane was cleared in the same way and the dock quickly emptied. As the job was finished the non-duty watch were allowed ashore; these men went to Times Square and other such interesting places. We also went to good eating places for a 'bust up'.

We went back to the ship and the next day sailed south to Norfolk in West Virginia. Our job was then to load with American *Avengers, Hell Cats, etc* preparing for the big push against the Japanese. The loading of these planes went ahead in reverse order to the unloading of the foreign planes. Each had its own position marked out and each filled that space. What space there was had already been allocated – beside the lift, lower deck and flight deck were full. We then moved south to the Panama Canal; it was to be an experience, the laden ship going through; I was to be amazed. The first thing was to position small engines on the rail track which ran the distance of the canal. By securing, with strong hawsers, the ship to the engines, a strong lashing was made and we were ready to move. I cannot remember how many ties were made, how many engines on either side, or how many times the track went up and down, but it did and kept the ship upright. As we came out the ship headed across the Pacific Ocean to Australia, the last part of our journey.

Henry Marshall,   Lincoln

During my war service I was attached in turn to the Australian AIF, a South African Tunnelling Company, the Indian Army, a Greek Brigade, the Palestine Buffs and a Canadian Artillery Battery and was stationed at Cairo, Jerusalem, Damascus, Beirut, Homs, Aleppo, Dier ez Zor, Alexandria, Sollum, Tobruk, Tripoli, Sicily, Italy and Austria – which was where I met the Russians.

28

And a scruffy lot they were too. They wore wrist watches up both arms and one chap was fascinated by a cold water tap. He kept turning it on and laughing at the sight of water pouring out. At night they lit huge bonfires of bombed timber and sat around drinking vodka. They welcomed us with open arms and asked how long it was since we'd had a woman. They offered to get us a 'Frau' and they were rather disappointed to learn that we didn't rape women and that we could be shot for rape in the British Army. They signalled that we should join the Russkis and live life to the full according to their standards.

We sat and got pally with the Reds for two or three nights and then one night when we joined them they were strangely quiet. There was no open arms or vodka and they were very surly. I for one did not like this attitude and decided to go back to my billet. Two other mates came with me and as we walked away one of the Reds shouted something. I turned round and saw that he was pointing a machine pistol at my back. We continued to walk away expecting to be shot at any moment but no shots were fired at us. We learned later that the Red Commissars had arrived to give the Russian troops an order direct from Stalin that they were not to be friendly with any troops from the West.

Albert Wood, Grantham

My husband went to a fête in Grantham while serving in the RAF and bought a ticket for a raffle. He duly won. What a surprise he got – the prize was a piglet. His home was a Nissen hut on an RAF camp! Luckily a farmer auctioned it for him for £3.

While serving in the WAAF my friend and I had a day off. We were due back at camp at 2359hrs so we took a ferry from Hull to Grimsby. After a long, tiring day we went to catch the boat back home, only to be told that the last one had already left. We went to the RTO and they took us to an army camp to spend the night. On arrival at the camp there was a dance going on, so we joined in.

Can you imagine the fun we had – two girls in blue (WAAFs) and all the rest in Khaki (ATS) – we were the belles of the ball. Alas, when we got back to camp, we had been AWOL and were placed on 'jankers' washing greasy pans for a week at our headquarters – Pearson Park. All good things come to an end.

Norah Gough,   Holbeach St John

'I had to collect the rear gunner.' Joan Highfield, RAF Waltham, 1943, and some of the "Radar Boys" mainly Canadian Wizard crowd.

I joined the WAAFs in 1942 and my first posting was to 100 Sqd at RAF Waltham, as a driver, where we could be anywhere on the air-field. I was once on ambulance duty with kites coming in after ops. I had to drive to this plane to collect the rear gunner, a bullet between the eyes. It was my duty next day to take him to RAF Binbrook to their mortuary.

J Highfield,   Lincoln

Tuesday 4 January 1944 saw me aboard *HMS Verdun*, a World War I destroyer. We were leading a northbound convoy from Sheerness to Methil in the Firth of Forth, and were travelling up the mine-free channel off East Anglia. The weather was fine and cold, the wind a brisk Force 6 and increasing. There were occ-asional snow flurries. At 15.10 we picked up a Mayday call from a B17 bomber about to ditch close to No 41 buoy. Verdun left the convoy, increased speed to 30 knots and despatched a signal;

'Aircraft crashed in sea at Buoy 41. Am investigating.' A Walrus flying boat passed overhead.

Within minutes the tail of a Flying Fortress could be seen slowly sinking vertically. We began to manoeuvre towards the two large circular dinghies which were lashed together, but the strength of the wind made this difficult as the dinghies were drifting so fast downwind. A line was fired towards them twice, on both occasions the white cotton cord was carried away by the wind. The third time the line was again blown fifty yards downwind from the dinghies. One of the aircrew jumped overboard and swam to pick it up and carry it back to the dinghies. Meanwhile the Walrus returned and dropped a five gallon oil-drum sized smoke float. We all hoped it wouldn't try that again!

By 15.35 we had hauled the dinghies alongside and lowered the scrambling nets. A huge patch of green fluorescent dye now marked the area. The ten American airmen scrambled and were helped aboard. Both dinghies were full of the green-dyed water and the men were also dyed a bright green. They were taken down to the wardroom and plied with various drinks. They stripped off their leather flying kit and were issued with the 'survivors kit' we carried, flannel trousers, sweater and gym shoes. I collected their valuables for safety and took down their names, ranks and numbers for the Log and Convoy report. My report reads: 'Rescue of American airmen from Fortress 26098 *Superstitious Aloysious*, 95th Bomb Group, Horham, Suffolk was effected in 29 minutes from the time they hit the sea until they were aboard *Verdun*'.

We rejoined the convoy and shortly afterwards a RAF air-sea rescue launch appeared alongside. The ten airmen were brought up and transferred across, not without some difficulty, as the launch was bouncing up and down some 15 to 20 feet. Back in *Verdun* the leather helmets, flying jackets, sheepskin boots and trousers had been divided out amongst us. Very welcome in the winter weather we were to experience.

Deryk Wakem, Deeping St James

left

'Monty came down from Luneberg.' Field Marshall Montgomery and Bandmaster Albert Howden on the quayside, 12 May 1945.

below

'With a nice piano and 200 bottles of Rhine wine.' Bill Baker (standing extreme right).

As a Co-op grocery assistant with very poor eyesight and a very moderate physique I never imagined I would become a soldier. However on 1 August 1940 I was called up to join the Pioneer Corps. After several special courses I was posted as Company Quartermaster Sergeant to 245 Coy PC, which was engaged in handling live ammunition. Everything from .303 rifle ammo to 25lb shells was stored in 70 miles of Elephant shelters along the lanes of Somerset and Dorset. June 1944 found me wading ashore in Normandy. I was amazed to see the REs already constructing a road leading from the beach using a Marshalls of Gainsborough diesel road roller. The gliders at Pegasus Bridge, the Bayeaux Tapestry, the bombing of Caen, the carnage of the Falaise Gap, crossing the Rhine on Swallow Bridge (pontoons) and aircraft flying over to Arnhem are all vivid memories.

VE Day found us in a Nazi Youth school at Rhiene on the Dortmund-Ems canal. This had only recently been vacated. With a nice piano, a sergeant who was an accomplished pianist and 200 bottles of Rhine wine in the cellar a very pleasant sing-song was enjoyed by all!

I joined the army weighing 9st 6lb and on demob weighed 14st, but I'm afraid it had not improved my eyesight!

Bill Baker, Lincoln

At the beginning of May 1945 I was a Bandmaster serving in the Royal Marines aboard *HMS Dido* and had just returned from Russia. We berthed at Rosyth and were granted a few days leave, but I had only been home a couple of days when a policeman appeared at my door. 'Return to your ship at once.' So back I went and within a day or so we were back at sea. Accompanied by destroyers and minesweepers we steamed straight across the North Sea, the 'sweepers bringing up mines frequently. A couple of German planes came over on 8 May and we opened fire. I think they were the last angry shots fired in Europe. On 9 May we steamed into Copenhagen, in company with *HMS Birmingham*, to take the surrender of the German ships and forces there.

We received a tremendous welcome from the local people massed there. I had the band on deck and among other items we played the Danish national anthem – all very emotional. When we went ashore later that day we were overwhelmed by the excited and exuberant Danish people, a welcome I shall never forget. On 12 May Monty came down from Luneberg to meet our ships companies and the Danish partisans.

In June we returned to Liverpool and embarked King George VI, Queen Elizabeth and the two princesses and took them on visits to Belfast, Isle of Man and the Channel Islands. So ended my six years of war where I was torpedoed, my ship was sunk by bombing at the Battle of Crete, I was also at the landings at Sicily, Taranto, Salerno, Anzio and the South of France, not to mention Arctic Convoys.

Albert Howden,   Horncastle

The Merchant Navy boys also served the country and so many were lost in the Battle of the Atlantic. I was lucky, serving as a radio officer for five years. During my long watches below in the North Atlantic I did cartooning which I used to illustrate on board for the ships newspaper. The captains of the different ships I was on used to appreciate a laugh because they believed it helped to keep up the spirits of the crew, many of them worrying how their wives and children were doing in the air raids.

I survived a bombing at sea and also an invasion of the North African coast. My ship was torpedoed 200 miles west of Gibraltar and when most of us managed to get picked up, our chief steward actually asked the Captain who was in charge of the lifeboat … 'Shall I serve the hot coffee now, Sir?' [*see frontispiece*]

Ray Drury,   Lincoln

I was called up into the Royal Navy in 1941 and remember the sinking of *HMS Hood* on 10 May that year, by the *Bismarck*. Out of sixteen hundred men aboard only three survived. The following song, to the tune of *Silent Night* was written about the tragedy:

"The HMS Hood *went down to the deeps.*
It was the sad news that made some mothers weep.
Sunk by the Bismarck, *one morning in May,*
With the guns all ablazing, she gave her display,
Now heavenly Father, look down where they lay,
Slumb'ring beneath the deeps."

I was courting during the war and sent money home to my girl every month. I later found out she had been with Italian prisoners of war and I asked for the money to be given back to a friend. She didn't, of course, and by the time I got back home she'd gone off with another British soldier and was never seen again.

Basil Pickwell, Boston

I returned to *HMS Europa* and was given another ship *HMS Curtana* an ex Grimsby trawler. We swept with magnets and 'Oropesa' on this ship as we had found the Germans were using magnetic mines. We did not yet know of the mines which were set off by the sound of propellers and were beginning to think that some of the neutral vessels going their own way were laying mines as so many ships were being blown up after we had swept the area. The Germans were very clever and were using magnetic mines which could be set to allow up to 24 ships to pass over them before the mine exploded.

The acoustic mine took a large number of our merchant vessels. We knew very little about them and I was sent to a small fishing village 14 miles east of Edinburgh where a fleet of 12 vessels with a minimum crew could watch for falling parachute mines. The position was plotted and the vessels were ordered out into the Firth of Forth and to move up and down over the position. If it was an acoustic mine the noise of the propellers would set it off. Six of the 12 vessels were blown up by the mines they went over. After many months an antidote was found to destroy these mines.

Verdun Willoughby, Grimsby

I was shot down in a Wellington bomber returning from a raid on Berlin during the night of 2/3 August 1941, and spent the rest of the war in POW camps in Germany and Poland. The following extracts are from the diary I kept:

Stalag 357, Thorn, Poland.

30 March 1945, Good Friday Half an issue of Canadian parcels arrived this morning. The news was excellent – Yanks at Paderborn 67 miles away.

4 April Sunny day, occasional showers, rather cold. American air raid in the morning, turned south over here towards Hannover. News good. Hopefully the end of the war this month.

6 April Panic during early morning to get us moved away. First party should have moved at 9.00am but not left at 4.00pm. We are second party, worse luck, but it may be easy to escape.

15 April My 25th birthday. Dogs barking and aircraft flying all night. Potato issue today – very cold morning – cold washing outside in spring water. Sugar all gone, but rumours of an issue to come.

19 April Happy and tragic day. Moved at 7.00am from Nastorf about 5km to Gresse where collected Red X parcels. Shortly afterwards were attacked by four Typhoons with cannon, rockets and guns. Our column of 500 and end of column in front were hit. Thirty dead and 48 wounded. Not pleasant to lie in grass and hear bullets zipping around. I was very close but escaped, only collected shower of dirt from bomb as I lay in hedge. Bad sights, several fellows cut in half. Many legs off.

John, fellow I knew from Leicester, amongst the dead. Tragic fate just as we were all so happy.

24 April Bad day and night. Felt very ill, ate nothing till evening. Many chaps ill, some pneumonia cases due to wetness. No news of moving, with Russians advancing too, there is nowhere to go.

2 May Albsfelde. First free allied man was an MP (British) in a jeep and smoking a fat cigar.

8 May Not far from Hamburg.

'We all disappeared to the nearest pub, had two free pints.' Jack Murfin.

Found Smithy. Had tea and biscuits together in canteen and purchased several things from gift shop. Stand by 12.15pm. Left barracks about 1.00pm for airport. Dozens of Lancs, a few Stirlings and one or two Dakotas. We left about 6.30pm and arrived at Westcott at 8.00pm. More cigs, tea and sandwiches then coach to Leighton Buzzard. We all disappeared to nearest pub, had two free beers, everyone friendly and sympathetic. Special train to Cosford. Soon got bed and good meal – bacon and eggs. No rationing here, have as much as you want. Saw MO about legs and have to have a few days in hospital. Suppose for best. Bed 5.00am.

Jack Murfin
submitted by Sue Macgregor, Skegness

I joined the WAAF in April 1943. I was a shorthand typist but they didn't want any of those so I was posted to Compton Bassett to learn Wireless Telegraphy. After a miserable time in this damp

'This damp spot.' No 3 Radio School, Compton Bassett. (from left) Sheila MacPhail, ?, Patience Gillieson.

spot trying to absorb the intricacies of Morse and electricity I was posted to the HQ of Technical Training Command at Reading – a metropolis in comparison with Compton Bassett, and then after a few months back to Wiltshire to the Bristol Flying School at Yatesbury.

The most lasting impression I have is that having lived in London during the blitz and buzz bombs, in Wiltshire the war could have been on another planet, although most of the pilots had been injured on active service and were recuperating. We also had a large number of Australians whose loving mothers sent them the most wonderful fruit cakes, something we hadn't seen for years, and we wireless operators were allowed to have a few crumbs.

Sheila MacPhail,   Lincoln

I was serving with the Ulster Rifles in France, and we had moved up close to the Belgian border around the end of August 1944 when this propaganda leaflet was dropped on us by the Germans. Their intention was to try and demoralise the British Forces but as far as we were concerned they did not stand a chance of winning the war! Although at the time I was single, a lot of my comrades were married and we all had a good laugh about it.

We were, of course, not supposed to pick up the leaflets as it was against military rules and we could have been severely reprimanded.

Arthur Biggs,   Grantham

MIRROR — WISE

A Precarious Story

Joan was in her room and just about to change because she intended to go to the Cinema with Bob. She had done that quite often since John, her husband had left for the front. — Why shouldn't she? Bob is a good friend of John's and he certainly wouldn't object. Everybody understands that Joan cannot always sit at home alone for years, without any companionship. —

Yesterday Bob came a little earlier than usual and entered Joan's room just as she was adding the last touch of rouge. She didn't mind his staying in there, they were really good friends — and so accustomed to each other.

As she rolled on her stockings, Bob told her all that he had done during business hours that day and then she noticed that the elbow of his jacket had a little grease spot, so she took it and cleaned it — What could anybody think wrong about that — among friends.

And then — — — Neither knew how it happened, she felt his strong body leaning gently against her — and then — they kissed — for a long — long while.

Joan was in a dream — — — she was feeling that marvellous something that she had missed for so long — it was so wonderful.

Then she opened her eyes — and there was that horror before her. Was it a dream — or was it reality?

She looked in the mirror and saw . . . . . . John! John in the arms of another! In the arms of Death!

But no, it was not John embraced by Death — — — it was YOU — and it was not Joan looking in the mirror but YOUR wife.

Joan is still alone.

And so are all the millions of other wives and girls.

But war goes on.

We shall defend our island ...

The threat of invasion and enemy attack resulted in the formation of units to defend the country should the worst happen. Although initially the Home Guard were inadequately armed and clothed they later became a well trained defence force, releasing soldiers to more active duties, while the Fire Service and Observer Corps were on duty and in action through the whole war.

*

I worked on a farm at Croft, near Skegness during the war looking after six horses for 30/– a week. I was in the Home Guard and we had to patrol the front after 7pm each night. One week we patrolled from Jackson's corner to the Pier and the next week from Gibraltar Point to The Vine. I recall the Germans bombing Friskney and heard about them bombing Kirkby-on-Bain and hitting the wood, thinking they had bombed Coningsby.

George Bell, Grantham

I joined the Royal Observer Corps in the latter part of 1943 and served at the Hackthorn post which was on the eastern side of the village about 100 to 150 yards onto an arable field. Many mornings when aircraft were returning from bombing raids I plotted them on their way back to bases in northern Lincolnshire and Yorkshire. Many aircraft were in dire trouble, engines out of action and fuselages with parts missing, but with the help of the ROC they usually made it back to base. The gratifying thing to me and other Corps members was when we were paid a visit by the crews of those aircraft to say thank you for helping them. One crew that gave us a call were unable to make contact with their base or anyone else because their radio had been blown away, but with our help they made it home.

Roy Grayson, Bracebridge Heath

We had a flower/fruit farm at Algakirk and had two men billeted on us to work on the farm. There were quite a few invasion alarms in our area and I remember them blowing up various bridges on the marsh.

Doris Watson, Boston

My son Richard was born during the war. I was in the General Hospital as the planes were flying over. My husband worked at Holland's but was also in the Home Guard. They used to congregate in our house every night then go marching off. He was guarding the docks two nights a week. We used to have three Sten guns and about 600 rounds of ammunition in the house.

Minnie Blakey, Boston

We had Home Guard training sessions one evening per week – arms drills, gun dismantling or first aid. We had Sunday meetings every week – either manoeuvres with C Company or a line-up and kit inspection. We had night manoeuvres three or four times a year and weekend camps perhaps twice a year, all with C Company which was made up of Castle Bytham, Little Bytham, Witham-on-the-Hill and Edenham platoons. When we had to go anywhere we'd meet at the village pond and pile into Tom Webber's lorry. It was open and you had the choice of sitting on the steel floor or standing up.

Night manoeuvres lasted from about 8pm to midnight. I particularly remember one was with the Red Berets, the Airborne Division, who were stationed at Grimsthorpe Park. We had thunderflashes to simulate hand grenades and to save rummaging for matches we had sandpaper brassards to strike the things on. It came on so wet they got soggy and wouldn't work. It got to midnight and then we discovered that the Red Berets, to liven things up a bit, had got real Molotov Cocktails and were throwing them at us! It was a bit nasty of them really.

Alan Crawford

submitted by Teresa Crompton,   Castle Bytham

I worked for an insurance company which dealt with War Damage and War Risks Insurances so this was taken into account when I had to register. I was called up therefore as a part-timer in the National Fire Service. We were supplied with uniform, steel helmet and a different gas

'Oh, not you again.'   Kath Ellis (right) with her aunt Mary Wright, WAAF.

mask, which we had to try after going through the Gas Chamber without one, which was most unpleasant. I was attached to HQ control room which had been built onto the rear of a house in Spilsby Road, Boston; the house was used as offices, sleeping accommodation *etc*. I went on duty every sixth night from 8.00pm to 8.00am and latterly every tenth night. Unfortunately the siren went on a number of nights when I was on duty and so some of the full time members nick-named me 'Siren' and when they saw me report in they used to say 'Oh, not you again. We won't have much peace tonight'.

Kath Ellis,   Skegness

I was in the Home Guard for much of the war and remember the invasion scare when certain bridges had to be blown up. One near Midville church was mined and a soldier who was not a local man didn't know and was blown up. He was buried in Midville church yard. I was on duty at Simonshouse near Old Leake station, about a quarter of a mile away, at the time and could hear bits of brickwork dropping into the drain.

On another occasion I was on duty with Colin Wood guarding the pumping engine at Old Leake. We had to challenge anyone who came down the road. At about 2am a figure appeared. I challenged him, 'Come forward and be recognised'. It turned out to be a soldier who had had a night out with some local girls and was having to walk back to Coningsby.

Morriss Gosling,   Boston

'Come forward and be recognised.'   'A' Company 1st South Holland (Boston) Home Guard, early 1940. Morriss Gosling back row 3rd left.

Make do and manage ...

While the Forces fought the war housewives battled against other problems to ensure that home life carried on in as normal a way as possible, although it was sometimes badly disrupted as strangers were billeted in empty rooms, and enemy action destroyed house and home. The need to produce and import war materials meant a reduction in consumer supplies, extra care with clothing and makeshift, sometimes unusual meals – and rationing. This did not, in itself, mean shortages. It was simply a means of distributing limited supplies evenly and while some people received less than they had been used to, others enjoyed a healthier diet and more food than ever before.

*

My fiancé and I had just got engaged and we were visiting some friends when war broke out. It was a lovely autumn weekend. I was just starting my training as a psychiatric nurse at Rauceby Hospital. The first week back at the hospital the sirens went and all the patients had to be taken down to the corridors underground for protection, which gave us very good practice when it was done. Very soon afterwards rumours abounded that the hospital was to be evacuated and was to become an RAF hospital. Meanwhile the last part of my training was completed and knowing that call-up was imminent, we got married; and before our anniversary my husband was called up. I was then expecting a baby and so started a search for safety pins, baby powder and all a child needs, which had become very scarce. When she was born the church bells rang out for the first time for El Alamein. My husband was home on embarkation leave and left when she was two days old. For months there was no news of his whereabouts until a letter came letting us know in a roundabout way saying 'Trixie our dog likes a bone, but I don't'. He was in Bone in North Africa.

Mavis Stimpson,   Ancaster

I ordered a cot when I became pregnant but nine months later the cot still had not arrived so my baby had to sleep in the bottom drawer. The baby had its own gas mask, a box that the baby fitted into.

Mabel Broughton,   Boston

My husband was in the building trade and was sent to work on Scampton aerodrome. We took a room on the first floor at 75 Carholme Road, Lincoln. The landlady lived in the kitchen and the rest of the rooms were let off as bed-sitting rooms. Our kitchen was a cupboard under the stairs which was shared with another couple and a single man also in other rooms in the house. We had a tiny gas cooker and an even smaller sink. However it was clean and comfortable and we all lived and managed amicably with never a cross word. At one stage the landlady left to live in another town and left me in charge to collect and forward the rents and deal with lettings *etc*.

The wife of a Lancaster navigator lived in one of our rooms and I shall never forget the morning they came to tell her he was missing. She was heavily pregnant and sobbed uncontrollably. She left soon afterwards. I always hoped she had a son to comfort her but such was the 'here today and gone tomorrow' attitude to life that we did not keep in touch.

It was an interesting sight to me to see a lady funeral director who lived nearby, she dressed in a top hat and tail coat and drove the hearse.

Rationing did not seem too hard to endure. Although we missed things like bananas and endless chocolates, we were never hungry, just tired of the endless 'making do'. Our tricks for spinning out food were endless. I could never fancy the horse meat sold uphill with its thick, deep yellow fat, neither did I like the whale meat though some of my friends ate it. I liked the dried egg which was issued and made lovely scrambled egg with it.

Herbal cigarettes were horrid and smelt like burning haystacks. The beer was very weak and a good thing too considering the amount the airmen drank.

Stockings were scarce and brown leg make up was used on bare legs. A line was drawn up the back of the leg with eyebrow pencil to represent the seam, which was the fashion in stockings. Even the little dots were drawn at the back of the ankle – quite a work of art trying to get the supposed seams straight. We also melted down lipsticks when they were nearly done and poured several into one old case to make one good one, which always came out a new colour and was quite exciting. A matchstick was held over the outside of the slot in the case until the melted lipstick set, which did not take long.

Betty Kirkham, Hogsthorpe

When my fiancé was on leave we went courting up Greetwell Rd. We came to a guard post and were challenged. My fiancé was alright – he had his ID card. I hadn't got mine, so had to present myself to the police next day and explain what I'd been doing in the dark! I was so embarrassed and had to tell them I was courting. We got engaged on Prison Rd, beneath the searchlights, in 1940.

Mary Watson, Lincoln

It is difficult to pick out the most outstanding memories of the war. Many people will recall, as I do, the sound of neighbours sweeping up shattered glass from their windows after an air raid, chattering like starlings as they recounted their lucky escape, or grieving over those who had been less fortunate. The nasty smell of the Anderson shelter in the back garden. If my sister and I got to it before anyone else in the family we used to send 'Totty Hardbake' the dog in first as the possibility of rats from the next door stables worried us more than the bombs!

'We used to send the dog in first.' Mary Cook (right) sister Ruby, and dog (circled) outside the entrance to their Anderson shelter.

There are other memories. Nights spent fire-watching in the old Primitive Methodist Chapel and going about in the blackout without ever fearing attack from anyone other than enemy aircraft. Making meals out of meagre rations and saving recipes from magazines. The kindness, comradeship and humour of ordinary people, the constant anxiety over friends and relations serving in the Forces. Being briefed by an imposing army officer on how to destroy the equipment used for relaying air-raid warnings, reports of unexploded bombs – especially the butterfly bombs which were scattered all over the town – and other local information over the Radio Relay Service where I was employed, one of my duties being the broadcasting of those items. It was at a time when there were strong rumours of a German invasion and it was considered vital that they should not have access to this form of communication.

Mary Cook,   Cleethorpes

During the wartime mum and dad kept a fish and chip shop. Friday and Saturday evenings were very busy times. We turned our living room into a restaurant. The supper room did well too. We had a lot of troops in. One lot sat down eating in the living room and another in the supper room. A third lot were standing in both rooms waiting to sit down. At night our supper room was used for fire watches all night. I remember the blackout and that we must not show any light. One night we made a slip up and the police banged on the door and said we were showing a light.

Dorothy Pickett,   Lincoln

'Mind your legs on the trunk' … a tin travelling trunk in the front hall? Yes, in case we needed to leave home quickly. Where were we going? … 'With our neighbours to their caravan at Donington on Bain.' This must have been during the phoney war period when all seemed almost normal to a little girl of almost five. I recall having to take a cushion to school together with a gas mask and for practice, as well as the siren sounding, we trooped down to the basement and sat on our cushions while Misses Curtis and Jameson somehow kept our attention. I do recall the foul tasting, brown sticky paper being stuck onto the window panes as an anti-shatter device.

There was no invasion, but a young mother and her daughter began travelling around the country. Where ever there were members of the forces stationed, local people opened their homes and let rooms to families of the troops. Trip one was on a musty, dusty LMS train from Louth to Lincoln, across the High Street and onto another train for Earl Shilton. From there, after a period at home we set off again for Long Eaton. Here we lived in rooms, and then in a house, and nightly the big guns boomed overhead. Following another spell at home mum and I went to Charlbury in Oxfordshire where life was quiet, with little or no wartime noises – just lots of army trucks and soldiers everywhere. I went to the village school which backed onto the lovely old house we lived in, owned by the village shoe-shop keepers.

I saw my first film at a camp children's party during our stay there, it was *Gulliver's Travels*. While we were living there our home in Louth was let to the families of personnel from RAF Manby. Letting agreements had to be renewed every six months so my mother and I had several journeys between Louth – London – Charlbury, almost always without my father.

We returned to Louth permanently in about 1944. For company, and to help others, my mother now let the dining room and one bedroom to RAF couples. I recall the nightly ritual of heaving the heavy blackout shutters into place on the windows then creeping outside to make sure not a chink of light was showing.

On Saturdays I emptied my doll's pram and with my mother collected salvage – newspaper *etc* from neighbours in Legbourne Road. During the summer many of us from school collected rose hips. If we collected some specific amount we were given a War Savings Certificate.

Christine Cook,   Dunholme

Rationing of food and clothes was inevitable, we were given books of coupons to obtain meat and fats *etc*. Milk was also rationed. It most certainly made us think of how to make the best use of what we had; we concocted meals no one had ever heard of before or since. We made Yorkshire puddings with dried egg, cakes with dried egg, we even fried dried egg when we got our bacon ration. Days without meat produced meals like steamed suet puddings filled with layers of what vegetables we could lay our hands on. 'Dig for Victory' was the password. The old gent who was our neighbour once shot a rabbit. He offered me some after he had cooked it but he had left all its 'innards' in so I had to decline!

Long queues formed everywhere for things that were not rationed but they were very scarce, often you queued up not really quite knowing what for, any addition to our diet was very welcome. Shopkeepers did their best to try and share out anything extra they managed to obtain among their regular customers. What a headache it must have been for them. One day in our local shop I asked if they had a cake – sometimes they got a few. The shopkeeper replied 'Sorry, not today.' and my young son, then three years old, asked 'Well have you got any under the counter?'. How quickly they catch on.

Margaret Mersy,   Market Rasen

Over fifty years ago it was a job to get a cigarette. We would tramp round the shops only to be told, 'Forces only!'. Fancy any shopkeeper saying, 'Look in the window before you come in'. What would the forces have done without our bullets and tanks. I am afraid them shops did not get much trade after the war.

Ruby Clark,   Manby

My mother-in-law lived with us for a while. She had brought her piano with her and this was used to have sing-songs with the service people. I got fed up with her living with us and she went home. Unfortunately she took her piano with her. This put paid to our musical evenings so I decided to buy a piano. When I went to buy one which had been advertised the lady asked what I wanted it for. It was a beautiful piano and when I told her what it was for she was delighted to sell it to me for the very reasonable price of £12. There was however one condition, the boys were not to play jazz on it. It had been her husband's piano and he could not abide jazz.

Despite everything my wife and I enjoyed the friendliness during the war. Many of the service men and women looked on our house as their home. Their parents would write to show their appreciation for all we did to help their children and my wife was heartbroken when the 'lads' finally left and went to wave them off on the train.

Tom Wood, Lincoln

During the early part of the war the number of garages licensed to sell motor fuel was drastically reduced in order that if there was an invasion the enemy would find it difficult to obtain fuel.

Rationed by means of coupons, people like doctors had coupons marked E for essential, trades people had SE for semi-essential, farmers F and service people on leave N. The coupon system made a lot of work, some customers choosing to bank the whole number of coupons with the Garage, others using them as they went along. Evenings were spent counting up the coupons which had to be sent off to obtain further supplies of fuel.

Enid Kisby, Wainfleet St Mary

I lived in Elder St, Bracebridge during the war. The family and I entertained Canadian Air Force boys stationed at Waddington. Some were very lonely being so far away from home. We liked light classical music and had lots of records. We invited them for a nights entertainment followed by supper. I cooked horseflesh steak and fried onions. The onions were from my husband's allotment and the steak was from Alec Christopher, the horsedealer, who had two shops in Lincoln. The air-force boys never knew what they were eating but it was always consumed and appreciated.

VE Day, the end of all the fighting, was celebration time so we decided to have a party; each house to contribute something to the spread. My contribution was six large bowls of home-made jelly, a kind of coloured pulp mixed with gelatine. It was a great success. Although most foods were rationed we had a great spread. After tea someone brought out their piano onto the road and we had a sing-song followed by a talent contest. As May 8 is my birthday it was one of the most memorable days of my life.

Dorothy Otter,   Lincoln

'Home-made jelly ... a coloured pulp mixed with gelatine.'
VE Day party, Elder Street, Lincoln. Dorothy Otter (circled)
and her daughter (sitting front row 3rd from left).

We had two acres of land and livestock so we were very self-sufficient and had also a pig which we kept for bacon. My grandma used to cut it up and saltpetre it in her very clean cellar after it had been killed. We had hams hung in the passageway in our bungalow and gave many a piece away to neighbours who had saved us their peelings. I remember once the pig got away and my father, grandfather and the person who was to kill it were all chasing it through the streets.

We all looked forward to the food parcels from Ireland and the USA because they had chocolate and tinned fruit in them. My mother used to exchange all her clothing coupons for sugar, tea and butter with other women.

Elvina Ibbotson,   Dunholme

I used to watch the planes flying over Boston and always waved if they were British. I remember just getting home one day when the door slammed. I thought the whole town was on fire but it was just light flares that the Germans had dropped to see where to bomb. It was very frightening, but also very beautiful.

Lily Clarke,   Boston

The basic ration of petrol gave one about 200 miles of motoring but this was removed in 1942 and only essential work for a car got any. As an agricultural contractor I got a fairly good allowance, including petrol for starting tractors. After a time tractor petrol was dyed and if any trace of it was found in a car engine you were in serious trouble. I have to admit I sometimes made journeys on a slim pretence of essential work.

Leslie Lunn,   Lea

I was living at Grimoldby during the war. One Saturday, at about 8am, a German plane, which had followed British planes back, was shot down by a gun at Manby crossroads. It came down behind Grimoldby church, on Somercoates Road. All the crew were killed and were buried in the churchyard. My boys went over to see the wreckage.

My husband worked at Grange Dairies and one lunchtime he was eating his lunch in the barn when the door was peppered by gunfire.

Florence Lidgard,   Louth

At the beginning of the war we lived in a three bedroomed house near the Park. I had two children. I did all my decorating with distemper – a powder which was mixed with water. We went all over the house and also stippled the walls using another colour and rubber squares to make a pattern.

We had tiled floors so we made mats out of old coats of different colours cut up into strips. When the rug was finished it was backed with hessian sugar bags to keep it firm.

We had a coal fire so we had to go through the park to get coke to help out with the coal. Sometimes we had logs.

I baked in the side oven and dried eggs were used a lot. I made a meal of potatoes by dipping them in flour and frying them.

We also used to queue for sausage meat and pork bones. I would cook the pork bones with the meat taken off; the juice from them was used to make stew with carrots, swede, soup powder and dumplings made of flour and lard. This was very filling. I made bread and butter pudding (from our butter ration) with raisins and custard for a treat.

Washing was hard work with the dolly peg to swish the clothes around and a gas copper for boiling them. I used Rinso and soap flakes for the woollens and carbolic soap to scrub overalls. I used to mend sheets by taking out the bad parts and putting the ends to the middle.

We had blankets up at the windows for the night. It was felt sheeting on a wooden frame.

I made clothes out of old trousers for the boys by cutting them down, the girls' dresses were bits of material. I used to buy wool with my coupons to make jumpers for the winter.

For entertainment we had the wireless 'Rented by Radio Relay'; we had hours of pleasure. I taught my children to read and we played games.

As my husband was away working on bomb sites in London I took in three families. They looked after themselves. I had just one big room for me and my children. We got along OK.

I used to be a 'runner' for a midwife. I kept a white towel, cotton wool and soap, so when necessary I lent them out.

In the summer we picnicked in the park. I had help to do the garden. As time went on we helped others and at the end of the war they went back to Manchester, Scotland, Wales; and two stayed in Lincoln.

On VE Day we had a street party, we all gave something to make it a lovely day, enjoyed by all. One never forgets good friends. Happy Times!

Mary Barwise, Lincoln

Keeping up appearances ...

The need to keep up the nation's morale was recognised early in the war and theatres and cinemas, some of which closed at the onset of war as a safety measure, soon reopened. Radio provided news, entertainment and many characters with whom the whole nation could relate, while amateur and professional drama and variety acts also flourished, sometimes formed from entertainers in the forces. The sound of bells for a victory was also joyously received.

*

We made our own entertainment. We loved the wireless and listened to the Big Bands and Vera Lynn. Everyone seemed to whistle and sing in those days and there were plenty of patriotic songs such as *Roll out the barrel, The White Cliffs of Dover* and *Hang out the Washing on the Siegfried Line*. The whole family listened to *Itma*. I liked it because it made my Dad laugh so much, it was very topical. Tommy Handley was a real tonic with his team of loveable characters including Mrs Mopp. Tommy would say, 'The shirts of today are the dishcloths of tomorrow'. Even I could see the significance. For a laugh we sometimes listened to Lord Haw-Haw, for no-one took him seriously.

When the snow came we would chalk a portrait of Hitler on the garage wall and throw snow balls at it. I very often sat drawing swastikas and I'm surprised I was not told off, but their design was intriguing.

Kath Marshall,   Nettleham

One of my most abiding memories is that of the 'Ack-Ack Players' formed by the 8th Reserve RA Regiment which was stationed in Cleethorpes for over three years. Because it was for most of that time an all-male regiment civilian female volunteers were warmly welcomed and I was a proud member. We were fortunate in having amongst our members several who were professionals in theatre, music and film making in civilian life, particularly George Tackaberry who produced, wrote and designed the scenery for most of our shows and had worked with the D'Oyley Carte Company and Ivor Novello; and Hector Leeman, whose stage name was Hector MacGregor, who had been the leading player in Windsor Repertory Company. They worked wonders developing the raw talent of the amateurs.

'Nobody loves a fairy when she's forty.' The 'Fairies Ballet' from 'The Sleeping Beauty', an Army Concert Party pantomime at Cleethorpes.

We performed in all kinds of venues; perhaps the most interesting was Haile Sands Fort in the Humber where we put on a show for the troops stationed there. We were taken out to the Fort at low tide in an army lorry, and seated beside the driver was a soldier with a large map. We were told he was there to guide us through the minefields so it was a little unnerving to hear him say to his colleague 'Left a little, no sorry, right. Slow down a bit, it's a little tricky here' and similar remarks. I don't know to this day whether the route was actually mined or whether he was having a joke at the expense of the female passengers. The interior of the Fort was very cramped and the toilet facilities primitive, but we gave our performance, only to find when it was time for us to leave that the tide had come in and we had to wait for it to go out again. Luckily our truck was parked above the water level.

On another occasion there was an alert when we were in the middle of a pantomime. There was a full house including many children and it was decided that they were safer inside than trying to get home or to a shelter. I was cast as the Wicked Fairy and was in the middle of my rendition of *Nobody loves a fairy when she's forty* when I had to contend with background noises of planes and gunfire and found myself ad-libbing comments on them to ease the tension.

Mary Cook,   Cleethorpes

Sunday night we always went to the pictures. It was lovely to have a treat. I don't think we should have got home if our boy friends had not taken us, the streets were pitch black, not a light shining anywhere. Everyone had to be so careful not to show a light.

Ruby Clark,   Manby

Sunday 15 November 1942 was proclaimed a day of thanksgiving and church bells were permitted to be rung on that day. Perhaps more than anything else they reflected the mood of the people, one of thankfulness, joy and hope. I did my best to get as many bells rung as possible.

We started at Gainsborough for the 11 o'clock service and decided that Gainsborough bells should be rung again in the evening, then went to the Isle of Axholme and rang at Epworth where people thanked us and we had free drinks at the Red Lion Hotel, Owston Ferry – where the bells were unringable, but we did our best, and Haxey where we were joined by one of the local ringers and rang for about an hour which was warmly received.

Returning to Lincolnshire we rang at Lea, Upton, Willingham and Stow. Here again we were warmly welcomed but of course it must be remembered that Church Bells had been silent since May 1941[1] since when they were only to be rung to warn of a German invasion. We stopped off at home for some refreshment then, as arranged in the morning, returned to Gainsborough to start ringing at 8pm. We rang for three hours and people were allowed up the tower to watch us ringing, a rope having been put across to keep them away from the ringers.

We finished at 11pm, came down the tower and witnessed the most amazing experience. The Churchyard was packed with people, some climbing up the trees to get a better view. They gave us a rousing welcome and I think this was the happiest day's ringing of my life.

Leslie Lunn, Lea

1. The ringing of church bells, other than as a signal for invasion, was banned from 30 June 1940 (not 1941). Although many people believe the ban was in force for the whole of the war, they were allowed to be rung on 15 November 1942 to celebrate the victory at Alamein and from 19 April 1943 the ban on ringing for services and special occasions was removed. Where bells did remain silent throughout the war it may simply have been because there was no-one to ring them. Ed.

Keep the war wheels turning ...

To service the needs of war industrial output increased rapidly and to supplement the workforce, and to replace men joining the forces, people were called up or directed into industry, agriculture, mining, nursing and anywhere where there was a shortage of workers. For many women this was their first experience of work out of the home. For some it came as a shock, while others enjoyed this new freedom and as the war progressed many factories employed a considerable number of women.

*

At the outbreak of war, if you were a married woman without children you had to do some form of war work. I was first sent to Thonock woods where we sawed up trees for pit props. This was quite pleasant as it was during the summer of 1940. Later I went to Marshalls, an engineering firm in Gainsborough.

My husband was working at another engineering firm and as we were on different shifts we had to leave each other notes. I was put in the inspection unit with another nine women under Mr Tommie Brooks. He was very nice and patient as we had never done anything like this before. I had to measure valve wedges for Rolls-Royce engines for fighter planes. The depth and width had to be measured to an accuracy of one four-thousandth of an inch and anything over this had to go to Mr Brooks who made the final decision. If the margin was small enough then it could be filed out. The girls on the machines were not pleased if the valves did not pass as they were on piecework, so sometimes we were not very popular. Often someone from Rolls-Royce would come down and inspect the work. They told us how important it was to get the work right otherwise men's lives would be at risk.

Hundreds of people worked at Marshalls and on Friday we could be queuing up for our money (£3 a week) for half-an-hour.

At first there were no breaks but later we were allowed half-an-hour each session. As I lived close by I was able to go home for lunch.

Vera Burton,   Gainsborough

My husband, who had run his own business, later went to work at Marco's, in charge of girls in the shell shop. They often got terrible dermatitis and went yellow from contact with the explosive. The Duke of Rutland's aunt and people from Culverthorpe Hall also worked there.

Joyce Hardy,   Grantham

In 1941 two events were to occur and change my life – I met my future husband and not long afterwards I got my call-up papers. I had always said that I would join the NAAFI and in spite of the person who interviewed me trying to get me involved in one of the other services, I stuck to my guns, and chose the NAAFI. On 5 November I found myself setting forth by bus to Louth and from HQ there to a camp at Louth Park in an army vehicle. It was quite an experience for the girl used to the peace of farm and country life and yet, as things turned out, they were some of the happiest days of my life.

I got a lovely warm welcome from Kathleen Evans, already established in Louth and from the manageress, a Miss Hulme. To begin with we lodged with a Mrs Overton on the Keddington Road which was very nice but a bit too far out – especially in the wartime blackout. The short cut was through a churchyard! So we moved into lodgings near the Park with a Mr and Mrs Taylor, again very nice. I soon took to NAAFI life, had a few days off in December for my wedding, then back behind counter.

I dare not relate all of the happenings but … . One dinner time we called into the guardroom and were happily chatting away to the Regimental Police when who should decide to visit – the Brigadier no less! Quickly we had to hide. I ended up covered by a Gas Cape and nearly smothered, my colleague hid under the table with a big cloth covering her. On another occasion we were being given an illegal lift home in an army truck which had to swerve to miss a pedestrian – we ended up hanging on for dear life. Perhaps my most outstanding memory is of the Padre, Captain Guinness – I think he was a member of the well known family of that name – a most likeable and charming man and very down-to-earth, with no ideas of grandeur or rank. I had served him with a cup of tea and someone rushed to give him a saucer, no doubt thinking this befitting for his rank *etc*. He simply handed it back, obviously not wishing to out-do the ordinary soldiers.

Sadie Lynch,   Cleethorpes

'You could always be sure of a cup of tea.' Accommodation huts at Stow Park and the ladies from the canteen.

I worked at Stow Park where lorries were loaded up with petrol and driven out to supply the airfields. I regularly visited Wickenby and it would take a whole day to get to such places as East Kirkby or Spilsby. There were about 50 to 60 drivers based at Stow Park. For the first week you followed someone else to find your way around and after that you were on your own. I didn't find this a problem as before the war I had delivered sand and gravel to where the aerodromes were being built.

Each lorry carried 2,000 gallons of fuel. When the aerodrome was reached it was usually WAAFs who had to connect up the pipes from the underground tanks to the lorry. Sometimes it was very difficult to unscrew the cap on the lorry and the driver would lend a hand although we were not supposed to.

Back at Stow Park, you could always be sure of a cup of tea from the canteen no matter what time of the day you arrived back.

George Taylor,   Gainsborough

The bathroom at Endsleigh was situated at the top of the house, four floors up – hazardous when taking a bath during an air raid, but handy for water during fire watching. One of my uncles and our next door neighbour, a lady, were on duty on the roof when incendiaries were falling all around. She asked what she should do with her bucket of water and was told to throw it. This she did – all over him! What my uncle said could have set a few more fires going. To add to her stupidity, when she refilled her bucket from the bath she pulled out the plug, thereby letting all the water away. She wasn't allowed on our roof anymore.

Margy Aitken,   Skegness

I lived in Grantham, but often visited Waddington to see my family. My brother was a postman and shoe repairer. Sometimes I would help him. I could do as many as seven pairs of shoes in an hour. He did the shoes for the village and the RAF and often had a batman appearing with shoes that needed to be done by the next morning.

Dolly Andrews,   Grantham

'I worked 60 hours a week ... but I loved every moment of it.'   Ruston & Hornsby's Boultham works, 1943. Mabel Wilkinson front row, 7th from right.

I started working in the 'Brass Gallery' at Ruston & Hornsby at Christmas 1940.   Not knowing what it was all about I felt a little apprehensive at first, but found everything very interesting.   I worked a big machine with a pulley to lift heavy component parts onto the machine and used a micrometer, working to a thousandth part of an inch.   During this time I worked 60 hours a week and when changing shifts after a fortnight on days, did the same on nights, but I loved every moment of it.   As time went on and air raids occurred we used to have to run outside for the shelters when the sirens sounded and sometimes found ourselves in them for two hours or more.

Mabel Wilkinson,   Lincoln

I went to London to be a Nanny after my fourteenth birthday, where I worked until war was declared.   I then trained at the Mid-land Agricultural College learning all aspects of dairy farming, milk churning, curd and cheese making *etc* and then – I was placed on a farm working with horses!   Up and down the Wolds all day, long days and very tiring ones.   Most days a horse ran away, me included.

When we wasn't with horses we would be driving sheep all day – not a dairy cow in sight.

On threshing days you had to work in the 'chaff hole' until you learned something else.   Wages were 28/– a week with 8d an hour overtime, tax was 10½d, lodging 14/–, so not a lot was left over.

On Saturday night my friend and I and two conscientious objectors walked to Market Rasen and back, six miles each way.   We pooled our money to go to the cinema in the Market Place, the men had five Woodbines between them and we had a 2d bar of Fry's chocolate.

Edna Kent,   Market Rasen

I volunteered for full time service in 1940 and was called up by the Red Cross to Stamford hospital as they were expecting – but did not receive – casualties from Dunkirk.   After six months I was sent to Burley on the Hill to prepare the Hall as a convalescent home for service patients.   It was a very happy place but by 1943, there not being much real nursing there, I applied for a transfer to the WTS(FANY).   Although ostensibly a transport organisation few of its members were actually drivers.   Most of the girls recruited worked for all manner of covert organisations and had to be fluent in a foreign language.

After acceptance we were assessed as for the jobs most suitable for us – in my case a coder with a knowledge of French – and after initial training, began work with SOE at a secret establishment in Oxfordshire where agents were trained in the use of codes before being sent off into Europe.

Shortly before D Day an American OSS signals unit arrived nearby and eight to ten FANYs went to be in charge of their coders, who had as yet no experience of the war.   Meals were large and the American cooks OK!   Cigarettes and other goodies we hadn't seen for ages were readily available … I remember that time so well!   By D minus 2 messages to and from American agents in Europe flooded in and out and were usually checked and double checked for errors, but eventually they were piling up and we had to send them up to HQ in London (by teleprinter) without checks. We were totally exhausted by the end of these days but very proud to be part of such an important operation.

Pat Edmunds, Bourne

We all had to work. One year I helped at a nursery for London evacuees. They had oranges every day and at tea-time the staff had marmalade made from the skins and a large number of wasps. It was nothing to find two in a spoonful.

At college we gave blood, acted as casualties for emergency training – no make-up, just labels to say what was the matter with us. One boy volunteer aged about ten was very noisy and as we waited pretending to be a bus queue in the town centre we checked his label. It said 'decapitated' so we guessed he had started misbehaving before he was labelled.

Joan Shields, Stamford

'I'd led a fairly sheltered life.'
Bridget Robinson, WLA, 1943.

I had been voluntarily evacuated from the Lincolnshire coast in 1940 to North Yorkshire. When my job there became de-reserved I decided, being a farmer's daughter, to volunteer for the Land Army. My family had already returned to Lincolnshire and I asked if I might be posted there too.

So I found myself travelling by bus from Sutton-on-Sea, via Horncastle, towards Bardney where, at Southrey Lane end, I was met by Bob, the foreman at the Southrey depot of the Witham and Steeping Rivers Catchment Board where I was to work. He delivered me to the family with whom I was to live and where another Land Girl (a 'townie') had already arrived. I'd led a fairly sheltered life, having been at a girls' boarding school and then lived quietly with relatives, so my new life, as part of a real country family in a house with absolutely no mod cons, and with a dirty outdoor job, was quite a culture shock.

Our job was originally to be trained as drag-line (R-B excavator) drivers but we both finished up as drivers' mates, although another girl had already been taught to drive. These machines cleaned the drainage channels and sloped the banks, then levelled the spoil which they had deposited on the bank and field edges. We did drive the engine on a narrow gauge line set up on the bank of the Steeping River near Gibraltar Point, (travelling daily in a rickety van on cold, dark winter mornings) which pulled trucks of spoil and dumped it in the required place. Needless to say the trucks would come off the rails and would somehow have to be heaved back on again! We also had to clean and paint the machines when they came in for servicing – a cold, dirty, greasy job, and we never got rid of the smell of diesel oil. We also helped the men when they 'roded' the smaller drains, forking up from the water the weeds *etc* which they had scythed.

Our uniform looked very smart for walking out but was not very practical for work, especially the 'pork-pie' hat which had to be tied on with shoelaces! We wore dungarees and smocks, with plenty of layers underneath when it was cold and the inevitable turban or headscarf, stiff boots and mittens. I put on weight during my stay in the WLA – complete change of life-style and food, with plenty of fat bacon from the home-killed and cured pig and suet puddings. We had a good social life with whist drives and dances at the village hall, occasional dances at the nearby RAF camp, visits to the cinema (where we sat in deck chairs, the best seats at the Kinema in the Woods) Home Guard do's and social events connected with the church and chapel in the village.

I was lucky enough to be able to go home fairly regularly which really made my life in the WLA more tolerable, but there were some fun times; two vivid memories – trying to keep my balance on a man's cycle along the narrow path alongside the railway line from Southrey to Stixwould; and standing on the river bank at Southrey Station shouting "Bo-o-o-at, Bo-o-o-at", when Shotty would bring the ferry, worked on a chain, to take us across to the pub opposite.

Bridget Robinson,   Boston

There was nothing wonderful or brave about my war work as a nurse in and around London, only very hard work, frequently under difficult circumstances, with the stress of air raids, lack of good transport and the ever frequent loss of family, friends and colleagues.   I worked in London during the worst of the air raids. Many women didn't leave the city so our work went on, frequently walking from case to case.   We saw some ghastly sights.   However, out of all evil comes some good.   The myriad of little bug-infested houses in the east end were razed to the ground.

On one occasion I was making my evening visit to a doctor's wife who refused to leave London when the siren wailed.   I quickly got the mother and her new twin babies into the cellar (set up as a shelter) and I then realised that incendiary bombs were falling everywhere.   I gathered my wits together and got on with carrying

'Out of all evil comes some good.' Joan Crust with deprived wartime children.

buckets of sand from the landing into the false roof, and put the wretched things out just before the doctor arrived home. On reflection I realise I couldn't have carried those buckets up a ladder under normal circumstances. Thanks for good old adrenalin!

Joan Crust, Skegness

Extracts from a Lincolnshire Land Girl's letters home:

March My official month's training is now finished and all I've learned is to riddle potatoes! There's a very long clamp of them, covered with straw and soil, in the field behind the farm house and they have to be forked into the riddle by one man while another turns the handle on a large wheel at one side of the contraption. The 'tates' roll down the mesh, the small ones dropping through and out into a basket at one side, while the big ones fall over the end of the mesh onto a slatted elevator and two or three of us pick off the badly damaged or rotten ones. The sound ones go over the top of the elevator into one hundredweight bags which another man weighs off and then

'We get the sacks, one day potatoes, another day fertiliser.'
Rose Grace (carrying sack) and Ada Davis.

are loaded onto a trailer or lorry for transport to the station.

April   They seem to think my face fits, or at least I'm not too hopeless – I'm now learning to drive a Fordson tractor (Oliver).

May/June   We are busy with the hay making now. Tommy is cutting with a tractor-drawn mower with a cut bar that works outside the tractor width leaving the grass lying flat in a long row, and the next time round the tractor straddles this row. When it has dried on the surface we go along with our pitchforks (known as hayforks in this part of the country) and turn the rows to allow them to dry on the underside. Then it is gathered into heaps and loaded onto flat carts to be built into fair sized cobs as near as possible to where the stack will be. I think our method of stacking is a Scottish one. A tall derrick pole is erected, secured by four guy ropes. Attached to it is a boom, which can be raised or lowered of course and on it are pulleys over which runs a rope attached to a large grab. Tommy backs the David Brown up to the cob, a thick rope is drawn round the base of it, each end secured to the tractor drawbar, and the cob is pulled to the foot of the derrick pole. The man in charge there secures the grab into as much hay as possible and a horse hauls on the rope lifting the loaded grab. Someone on the stack among the five of us (frequently me, I'm not yet much good at stack building!) pulls a light rope fastened to the tip of the boom and brings it round so that the grab is over the stack and the man on the ground jerks his rope to open the grab and release the hay. You may imagine a bit of fun is sometimes had by releasing it above someone working on the stack.

Joan Brandon, Sudbrook

I had got myself a job on the Co-op milk round in Scunthorpe, starting with a hand barrow and later moving to a round run by Olga Green using a horse-drawn cart. I was to remain on this round for a long time, delivering over 600 pints every day and sometimes over 1000 at the weekend. We often worked 10 hours a day, sometimes starting and finishing in the dark, for this I received the princely sum of 30 shillings.

The horse we used to pull the milk float was black, fat, very old and wouldn't go very fast. We used to call it a lot of un-complimentary names although its real name was Jet! Before we started our round each day we had to harness the horse, a task which filled me with foreboding as I was frightened of putting the bit in his mouth. At the end of the day we had the whole process to reverse before the stable men took over. Once the harnessing was complete we had to pull the cart up to the loading gantry and back the horse into the shafts. The candle-powered lanterns had to be attached one to each side of the front and one to the rear before being checked for sufficient length of candle and lit. When the day's deliveries were over that was not the end of it. As well as un-harnessing Jet we also had to unload the cart and count the empties and breakages as part of the checking in process before entering the office to cash up.

'We had to harness the horse.'
Ruby Horton, 1940.

Ruby Horton, Scotter

During my work at Ruston & Hornsby I had Army and RAF officers visiting me. They were taken round the office by my chief then stopped at my desk. This was strange to me and they picked up and looked at one of the drawings I had. The RAF officer grunted and put it down quickly and they went away. The drawing was one of a good batch which I had been presented with earlier. They were all German. My job was to get the materials to make the objects on the prints which meant they all had to be translated into English. I complained and said I was unable to translate them and was told 'Go and get the German books you need and we will pay for them'. In the drawings were a diesel engine, virtually equivalent to a Paxman engine (Paxman's were part of the Ruston organisation so they were passed on) and another item, a gearbox quite unknown to us. It was designed to reverse from the highest speed forward to the same speed reverse immediately. When the first gearbox was built it was tested in a small indoor 'lake'. This was a weapon we needed for the attack across the English Channel. Small vessels could run out of the sea onto the sand beaches, open their doors, unload and then reverse at full speed back into the sea allowing others to follow them.

Jack Hawkins,   North Hykeham

I started to train as a nurse in 1941 but after about a year I became very ill. They thought it was rheumatic fever and I was sent home to recover. There the doctor found I had arthritis in my knees and other joints so he finally advised me to give up nursing, but the hospital had to release me from my contract and weren't very pleased. A contract was a contract and having signed on for three years you were expected to stay for three years, no matter what! By the time I had recovered, in October 1942, they were opening day nurseries in Grantham so I applied for, and got, a job there.

The nurseries were open from 7.00am to 7.00pm and often later if mothers 'forgot' to fetch their children. The cost was 1/– a day and that included breakfast, dinner and tea. We worked two shifts, either from 7.00am to 4.30pm or from 11.00am to 7.00pm. The early shift started with lighting two stoves, one in each room, and they were very cold in winter as the buildings were prefabricated with no insulation. All the mothers were out at work, many on munitions, and most husbands were in the forces. Some were single mothers and the nursery was their salvation. A lot of them did not know how to look after children properly and we tried to teach them. Some babies returned in their prams at 7.00am exactly as we sent them home at 7.00pm the previous night, but steaming from un-changed nappies!

Having lit the fires and welcomed the children, breakfast was served, cod liver oil *etc* given and then toilets. One little boy called Ernie Bee came racing back shouting 'Aye Miss, me trousers is gone down the lavvy. I dropped them in, pulled the chain and they went'. Poor Ernie had to have nursery pants that day. My next job was to tooth-comb all the heads, clean up the ones with nits and lice and try to catch the fleas before they jumped onto me, and often they did just that. All the children in the baby room were bathed every day and the toddlers had a bath once a week.

On tough little boy threatened to call me 'what our mam calls our dad' and he did! Wow. I thought I'd heard some language in hospital but that outshone the lot. We certainly learned a lot about life and children!

'Poor Ernie had to have nursery pants.' Children at Dysart Rd nursery (left to right) Jackie Henderson, Ernie Bee, Pattie Undy, David Pretty, Christine Batch, Pauline Batch.

Junior nurses took it in turns to do the laundry, *ie* washed and boiled all nappies and towels, washed all overalls, pants *etc* – no washing machines, it was a sink, copper and wringer – and then the ironing. After work we had to do at least one night a week on voluntary war work and I helped to man the ARP post at the hospital where we had to sleep.

Barbara Teague, Harlaxton

Toys were very scarce in the day nursery, just a few puzzles and educational toys were supplied and the Canadian Red Cross sent soft toys. We also had a sand-pit and later, at St Catherine's, a slide, but most of the toys were made from scrap. Being taken to the dump by a very forceful lady who came from time to time to inspect us, we brought back empty tins and boiled them in the copper and then painted them. I can't remember how we got the paint and I am sure it was not lead free! Some of these tins made stacking towers, others we filled with clothes pegs for the children to play with. We used to thread cotton reels and thimbles on ribbons for rattles and shaved old toothbrushes then softened and bent them to make rings for the babies to chew on. The most popular toys were beer bottle cases. These were originally begged and then painted green to use as extra seats but could be anything the imagination ran to. At Christmas the tree was decorated with beads strung on wire and painted egg shells cadged from family and friends as we had only dried egg.

Although we only had dried egg we actually did quite well for food, or so we thought then. Fish was not popular and was only eaten when it was disguised as meat by smothering it with brown gravy sauce. I remember cakes made from cake crumbs rolled up in sweetened cocoa sent by the Canadian Red Cross. They also sent tins of apple jelly which was served one lunch time and all the children fell asleep very quickly afterwards. When we had our own lunch we discovered why – the jelly was fermenting!

Janet Spratling, Ipswich

VE and VJ embroidery rescued from a Grimsby jumble sale.

When the lights go on again ...

After six years of war victory was celebrated as never before with strangers hugging and kissing and street parties despite food shortages. The end of the fighting did not always mean that the troops returned immediately but at least there was now a chance that they would return safely and both VE and VJ day were as much a communal sigh of relief as a thanksgiving.

*

I lived at Hemingby at the time. A few days previous to VJ Day itself I was admitted to the local hospital with a dreadful attack of pneumonia. Temperature so high, I was fitted with a thermal vest or jacket to sweat it out of me, to no avail. On the night itself I remembered in between numerous bouts of fading away and coming to, music in the distance, which I found out afterwards was the Town Band passing through on its way to the Market Square.

Penicillin came into being about this time, but was unobtainable locally. My doctor contacted an army team stationed at Grimsby and requested help, which they were able to give. A few doses brought things under control and at the end of six weeks I was allowed home, thermal vest still intact, which was to be kept on until it disintegrated, which in due course it did.

Kathleen Dickinson, Horncastle

On VE Day I was in Leicester and we had a high old time going through the streets, in and out of the pubs, in a mile long Conga. No one went to bed that night, we carried on right through until morning.

I married my sweetheart in July 1945 and we spent our honeymoon in London. When we woke up on the morning the war was declared over the noise was unbelievable. We went to look out of the window and across the streets of Kilburn people had hung effigies of Hitler, Mussolini, Goebbels and Goering. They had set fire to them and everyone was shouting and cheering, it was a sight that has remained with me and I won't ever forget it. That same evening my husband and his friend who were in a camp at Upper Norwood came home via Piccadilly Circus and the celebrations there were out of this world. His friend's wife and I said 'Will you take us back there?'. 'No way!' came the reply in no uncertain terms so we celebrated by going to the pictures to see Ronald Colman in *Lost Horizon*.

Joan Cropley,   Pinchbeck

We heard on the 8pm news on 7 May that VE Day would be tomorrow and so we had the day off work. I went to communion at Skirbeck St Nicholas Church at 7.30am. I went shopping in the morning, listened to Mr Churchill on the radio in the afternoon then went to Boston Fair with my friend Hilda and in the evening with my Airborne soldier friend, John. We went all round the fair and I went on all the rides and stalls meeting various other friends on our travels. On our way home just rounding the corner into Skirbeck Rd, someone had pushed their piano out onto the pavement and so we joined in the singing and dancing in the street and I didn't get home until 1.00am.

VJ Day was announced at midnight on 14 August so once again we did not work on 15 August and some of mother's friends came and we had a tea party and all went to church in the evening.

Kath Ellis,   Skegness

I was a girl of 14 years, living at 65 Tower Crescent, Lincoln and there was a lot of excitement when VE Day was announced. The housewives all got together and they arranged a street party and we really flew the flag for Great Britain. It was a lovely occasion. In the evening I remember Mr Brammer who was then a Special Constable. He used to have his own concert party called Arthur Brammer's Follies, of which I was member. All the men carried his piano out onto the Green and we all had a good old sing song.

Blanche Ward,   Ashby-de-la-Launde

'We really flew the flag for Great Britain.' Tower Crescent
VE Day celebrations, Blanche Ward (circled)

I remember sitting in bed listening to the radio when there was an announcement. As a child of 10 it really didn't have much impact on me and as it was my birthday on 8 May, that was uppermost in my thoughts. Then lots of things started to happen.

My mum told my older brother and her younger sister, Aunt Doll, to get up and get dressed. As it was around midnight this was to me quite scary as I had never been up this late. Then, as if by magic, everyone in our street was also up and out. Lights were switched on and curtains drawn back. Mrs Burrow's son had turned up the gas lamps and with help from friends pulled his

79

mum's piano out of the front room into the street. Mr Howard from the corner shop brought out a barrel of beer and a crate of pop and even Mrs Howard, who always moaned a lot, gave us a box of penny packet crisps.. Everyone was singing and dancing and we all joined in and did the Conga. Then as I was stood near my mum she said 'What a wonderful birthday present for you.' – and for the rest of the street celebrations I really thought that everything was for my benefit. I was so excited, as I had never had a birthday party before, and I stayed excited for a week at least, before I realised that it hadn't been my birthday party at all, but that peace had been declared over Europe. But we had a wonderful night nevertheless, also a great street party.

Madge Dorr, Sturton by Stow

I was at Undini in Italy when I heard peace had been declared. The troops were beginning to become quite disillusioned as mistakes in planning by superiors had been made. My first reaction was that I could go home, everyone was quite elated, the Union Jack was unfurled and the soldiers' movements were no longer restricted. We celebrated, and were drunk on Canada whiskey for three days.

Leslie Chambers, Lincoln

On 7 May I was helping to decorate the Smoke Room at the Butcher's Arms public house at Navenby. We had got the ceiling and walls distempered and the furniture and settles washed down with vinegar water to remove drips and old polish, when we saw people beginning to queue up outside the front entrance waiting for the six-o-clock opening time. We were too busy to listen to the radio to find the war in Germany was over. This was my first day working for the tenants of the pub, and as I had a six year old son at school in Navenby, he used to come and wait for me to finish. But we never got finished, we didn't get anywhere polished as I had to leave because the pub was so busy and I had to get my son off the licensed premises.

So we had to go home and I heard the news on our wireless, and so to bed after a meal. In the middle of the night I heard stones being thrown up at my bedroom window. I got out of bed and opened the window and found it was my husband who I thought was far away in Germany. I hurried downstairs to let him in and he told me he knew the war was over before he left. He had got a fortnight's leave. In the morning I cycled to Navenby where I shopped and the shop was locked and trimmings were across the street. I had gone to get my husband's ration card and I went to the shop window and held it up and they couldn't get the door open quickly enough to serve me, they were so proud of him.

As we had left our four year old daughter in Lincoln with my Dad and stepmother we got the bus to Lincoln to go and get her. My husband was the only member of the family in the Forces and my Dad was so proud he kept buying quarts of beer from the off-licence opposite. They were sitting outside the house on a low wall and Dad kept telling everybody, 'this is my son in law and he has just come on leave from Germany'. Everybody was so excited that day, I don't think our two children realised what all the excitement was about. That night we went up to the top of the South Common where a huge bonfire was

'This is my son-in-law.' Gunner Raymond Beesley, 4th Regt RHA.

lit. When it was time to go home my husband found out he had lost a fluorescent brooch, a windmill some Dutch people had given to him, so that took a bit of a shine off the day.

Phyllis Beesley,   Lincoln

We were working on the land picking potatoes when we found out the war had finished. We just threw our 'tatty' baskets up in the air and started singing. We nearly frightened the horses into a stampede. That was work finished for that day and the next thing we heard was the church bells ringing, which sounded lovely after they had been silent for so long.

Eve Dawson,   Boston

We lived in Kirkby Street in Lincoln, close to Sincil Drain. At the end of the war we had a huge street party. I was not quite four and had never experienced anything like it in my life. Long trestle tables covered with white linen were set in the middle of the road. There were few cars about in those days so this did not cause a traffic hazard. The children sat on benches and there was food, oh so much food! People were at last prepared to use up the tiny stocks they had put away 'in case the worst should happen'.

And then a walk up the High Street after dark. I shall never forget my absolute bewilderment at seeing the Ritz Cinema lit up with coloured lights, nothing by today's standards, but something I had not seen or even dreamt of before.

Alan Middleton,   Lincoln

Bronchitis kept me in bed on VE Day, so I watched from the bedroom window as the other children and the neighbours were all out in the gardens. Someone went to town and bought some red, white and blue ribbon for my hair and a flag for my bike. A young RAF couple billeted next door to us had a very old car and, wrapped up in blankets and an eiderdown, they took me out up to Kenwick Hill to see the floodlighting of Louth Parish Church spire. It was magic, there looked to be two spires and a 'V' sign appeared at times. Bedtime thoughts on that night, …there's no need to have my outdoor coat on my bedside chair, is there?'.

Christine Cook,   Dunholme

My service was as a pay Corporal for an assault squadron, Royal Engineers. The squadron was equipped with Churchill tanks (AVREs) mounting Petards and our principal role was breaching static defences.

In late April we were in tented accommodation at the edge of a wood just outside Luneburg. News of the cessation of hostilities came down from Regimental HQ to us on the wireless net and the rest of the day was spent at leisure in the squadron lines. During the war our squadron had been equipped with Sten guns. No one had ever fired his Sten gun! I well remember as the night went on – and festive rejoicing continued – the air was full of the sound of Sappers firing their Sten guns! I lay in my tent thinking what a pity to come so far and be wounded now.

'No one had ever fired his Sten gun.' (standing left to right)Jim Allwright, Les Whitbourne, Peter Olsen, (sitting) Doug Morris

Peter Olsen, Nettleham

When VE Day came I was a big girl then. I'd been out at work about six months, working at a café in Peterborough. They were rather hard people and, really, you had to toe the line. Everyone else had a day off, but we weren't terribly sure so, of course, I had to go into Peterborough to find out and yes, we were allowed a holiday.

We went round the town and saw the Americans. There were loads of them just around Peterborough and of course they were all in the town. We had a jolly time in the Market Place, I don't know where the music was coming from but we were dancing. We had a marvellous time. I just think everybody was so very happy.

I had a boyfriend at the time. He'd got a boat and we went up the river; it was getting dark. When I first saw those lights without the blackout, it really brought it home. It was really something magical.

Iris Cooper, Deeping St James

The cumulative effect of the war years resulted in personal ill health. On VE Day I was a patient in a hospital for Wrens in Vincent Square. We could hear the cheers, the bands and the singing. A nurse, describing the scene through the ward window reported that a GI and a British matelot were up a lamp post and singing *Lili Marlene*. In July I was posted to *HMS Demetrius* situated on Wetherby racecourse. On VJ Day I was proud to be the leading marker of a large contingent of Wrens marching past Leeds Town Hall. Our war was over.

Joan Brown, Skegness

'I was posted to HMS Demetrius.' Wrens and sailors rowing on the River Ouse, Wetherby, July 1945. Joan Brown came 3rd out of 12. Wrens were now allowed to wear civilian clothes at weekends.

The VE Day announcement brought the end of bombs so we were ready to give thanks and in the morning I remember going by tube train to Trafalgar Square and then to Westminster Abbey to attend a service of thanksgiving. As we walked down Whitehall my mother was not happy about her shoes – they were not at all comfortable and spoilt her freedom to enjoy the day. The shoes had hinged wooden soles and had been fewer clothing coupons than more conventional types; the navy blue suede and scarlet leather uppers were attractive and I think it was a gesture to our national colours of red, white and blue that made their being worn so appropriate on VE Day. I had a 'favour' in my jacket lapel, a little group of pom-poms in red, white and blue and many people had similar decorations.

Pamela Turner,   Sleaford

I was a sergeant in Burma for eleven months and was on a Dutch hospital ship some days out from Bombay when the captain announced on the radio that hostilities had ceased in Europe. We would however still continue under blackout because he was afraid that certain U-boat commanders might not have got the instructions, or might not obey them. To celebrate the day, each man on the boat was issued with two bottles of beer.

Ivor Penny,   Uffington

I was in a village in Belgium called Doel, on the banks of the river Scheldt running a small signals outpost in the RAF. When the news came through that the war was over, the commanding officer, Fl Lt Atkinson, authorised the free issue of cigarettes, beer, sweets and I don't know what. Everyone was excited and the villagers were mingling with us RAF people and everyone was making whoopee. It was hard to believe that after so long it was all over at last.

Stephen Hare,   Stamford

I was 17 when the war started. I worked in the landing craft recovery units and was in Arnhem at the time of VE Day. I had been sent there to repair the boats but these were not required as a pontoon bridge had been built. I remember seeing lorries loaded with Nestlés condensed milk being driven towards Belsen.

When I returned to England I was sent to North Devon, preparing to go to India but VJ Day ended all that. On VJ Day I was in Instow. The local pub had run out of beer so we had scrumpy straight from the wood – the next two to three days were a bit of a blur!

Brian Edwards, Grantham

When 8 May dawned we were not sure that it was to be VE Day. However a blast on Miles' Woodyard buzzer during the morning confirmed indeed that it was and we felt able to celebrate for a short time, always bearing in mind that there was still a war on in the Far East. I was probably conditioned to this reservation because I had worked with the Americans for two years at Walcott Hall and their thoughts were very much in the Pacific.

The day turned out fine and sunny. We were living at Wothorpe and had a prematurely born six week old baby daughter. In the afternoon we put her in the pram and brought her down to Stamford for her first outing there. We made for Broad St and joined the crowd assembled there, milling round an impromptu celebration. We met several friends who had their first glimpse of our daughter before returning home to Wothorpe. There had been an egg ration that week and consequently we were able to have a celebratory egg-and-chips meal with the chips being cooked in margarine.

About this time we invited Jake, an American serviceman, to our home. Jake was of Syrian descent and was the epitome of the description 'a bear of a man'. He picked up our 6lb daughter when I was afraid to hold her and he picked her up with a practised hand. Later he showed us his family photograph: mother, father and 14 children. Jake was the oldest and had handled his siblings over the years.

It was with Jake and his fellow servicemen that we spent VJ evening. It really was their celebration. We congregated in the

Stag and Pheasant in Broad St. Beer flowed liberally and in-hibitions were lowered and it all became very noisy. Some GIs were given a pint of beer and told to drink it without pause. If unsuccessful the depth of beer remaining in the glass was meas-ured and the equivalent length was cut from the drinker's tie. Some were down to the last inch below the knot. At this point a WAAF approached him saying 'You haven't lost your tie but you are going to lose your trousers!'. It was then that we saw fear on Jake's face. We, and I'm sure Jake, thought she would be successful in removing them but somehow, after much hilarity, he managed to extricate himself and it was time for another GI to have his tie cut.

Lawrence Tye, Stamford

I was stationed at RAF Wittering and on detachment to RAF Tangmere with the Air Fighting Development Squadron. In early June I was with a small team sent to Washington USA to carry out tactical trials with American aircraft, the latest captured Japanese fighters and the RAF Spitfire Mk14 with the Griffon engine. The trials commenced at Newark NJ but were discontinued following the dropping of the Atomic bombs on Japan on the 6th and 9th of August.

I was recalled to the UK on 14/15 August and was on my way home when the captain of the aircraft passed round a leaflet *(overleaf)* giving us the good news that the war had finally ended.

James Dorrington, Stamford

BRITISH OVERSEAS AIRWAYS CORPORATION

To PASSENGERS   PLEASE PASS ROUND

From CAPTAIN _POOLE_   Aircraft _AL603_

Time _23.00_ G.M.T. _____ Local

Our position is _310 naut. miles from GANDER_

Altitude _9000_ feet. Temperature _+5_ deg. Cent.

Ground Speed _255_ miles per hour.

Our Flight Plan estimated a _9_ hrs. _45_ mins. Flight.

Our estimated time of arrival at _PRESTWICK_

is _07.20_ G.M.T. _08.20_ Local Time.

In _____ mins. we should pass on our Starboard / Port

B.B.C. NEWS ALLIES ACCEPT JAPS OFFER
PROVIDING EMPEROR OBEYS ALLIED COMMANDS
AND GIVES NECESSARY INSTRUCTIONS TO CARRY
OUT POTSDAM DECLARATION CONDITIONS.
JAP AMBASSADOR IN SWITZERLAND HAS

Remarks: _NOW RECEIVED THE ABOVE OFFICIALLY_
FOR TRANSMISSION TO TOKYO NO CEASE
FIRE AS YET.

_____ Navigator.

Betty Kirkham, 1939.

Epilogue ...

1942 – 1945

I wonder if I'll ever know again
A night unbroken by an aeroplane?
A day without a bulletin,
Or someone asking when we'll win?

Will there ever be a building large
Which bears no sign of camouflage?
A seaside town where I may find
A beach that is not thickly mined?

And will I ever purchase what I please
Without a sharp request for "Coupons please"?
And will supply again exceed demand
Of fruits which now to us are banned?

Will cars and petrol ever be
The right of folks like you and me?
Will clothes and fags be free of tax
And beer contain the kick it lacks?

So many changes war has wrought
Our private lives now count as nought,
Though I may question things in rhyme
The answer lies with Father Time.

Betty Kirkham,   Hogsthorpe

Index of contributors